"In this slim volume, Pastor Hyde gently calls upon Christian parents and churches to place their children in 'the nursery of the Holy Spirit.' This helpful volume also offers practical ways in which moms and dads may 'parent in the pew.' I am grateful for this book and plan to get it into the hands of the parents and ministry leaders in my church."

—Todd Pruitt
lead pastor, Covenant Presbyterian Church, Harrisonburg, VA

"Many reasons are given for why children drift away from the church but perhaps the most important and least discussed—is the fact that parents do not teach them that church is important. And basic to that is making sure children are in the worship service and understand what is happening. Danny's little book will be a great help to parents and pastors as they reflect on how better to encourage little children to come to Christ."

—Carl R. Trueman
pastor, Cornerstone Presbyterian Church, Ambler, PA

The Nursery
of the Holy Spirit

Also by Daniel R. Hyde

A Well-Ordered Church: Laying a Solid Foundation for a Vibrant Church (with William Boekestein)

God in Our Midst: The Tabernacle and Our Relationship with God

God With Us: Knowing the Mystery of Who Jesus Is

In Defense of the Descent: A Response to Contemporary Critics

In Living Color: Pastoral Counsel on Images of Christ

Jesus Loves the Little Children: Why We Baptize Children

Planting, Watering, Growing: Planting Confessionally Reformed Churches in the 21st Century (editor)

The Good Confession: An Exploration of the Christian Faith

Welcome to a Reformed Church: A Guide for Pilgrims

What to Expect in Reformed Worship: A Visitors' Guide

Why Believe in God?

Why Should I Fast?

With Heart and Mouth: An Exposition of the Belgic Confession

The Nursery
of the Holy Spirit

Welcoming Children
in Worship

Daniel R. Hyde

WIPF & STOCK · Eugene, Oregon

THE NURSERY OF THE HOLY SPIRIT
Welcoming Children in Worship

Wipf and Stock
An Imprint of Wipf and Stock Publishers
199 W. 8th Ave., Suite 3
Eugene, OR 97401

www.wipfandstock.com

ISBN 13: 978-1-62564-832-7

Manufactured in the U.S.A.   07/23/2014

Unless otherwise noted, all Scripture is taken from *The Holy Bible, English Standard Version*, copyright © 2001 by Crossway Bibles, a division of Good News Publishers. Used by permission. All rights reserved.

Scripture quotations marked KJV are from The Holy Bible, King James Version.

All quotations of the Heidelberg Catechism, Belgic Confession, and Canons of Dort are from *The Creeds of Christendom*. Vol. 3, *The Evangelical Protestant Creeds*. Edited by Philip Schaff. Revised by David S. Schaff. 1931. Reprint, Grand Rapids: Baker, 1996.

All quotations of the Westminster Confession of Faith, Westminster Shorter Catechism, and Westminster Larger Catechism are from *Westminster Confession of Faith*. 1958. Reprint, Glasgow: Free Presbyterian Publications, 2009.

To Cyprian, Caiden, Daxton, and Sadie:

May your childhood be filled with
the joyful noises of Jesus.

". . . believers have no greater help than public worship, for by it God raises his own folk upward step by step."[1]

1 Calvin, *Institutes*, 4.1.5.

Contents

Foreword by Dr. John D. Witvliet | ix

Acknowledgments | xi

Abbreviations | xiii

Introduction | xv

1 Children's Church or Children of the Church? | 1

2 Children in Worship in Scripture | 16

3 Parenting in the Pew | 35

CONCLUSION A: Plea for Children in Worship | 55

Bibliography | 61

Scripture Index | 65

Confessions Index | 69

Foreword

CHILDREN ARE AN INDISPENSABLE part of the worshiping community, incorporated into the Christian community at baptism not as second-class church members to be merely tolerated, but as deeply cherished gifts of God to be embraced. They enter the church community as those called, like people of all ages, to "grow in the grace and knowledge of our Lord and Savior Jesus Christ" (2 Pet 3:18). And they enter the church community as both students, but also in an important sense as teachers and models, demonstrating time and time again the sheer grace of childlike trust.

For the past several decades, many North American congregations have pursued generationally segregated approaches to worship and church life. While motivated by a desire to tailor events to the unique needs, learning capacity and temperaments of each age group, this practice has often had the unwitting consequences of promoting the idea that worship should be remade in the image of each generation and of making cross-generational learning and fellowship much harder to achieve.

In this context, it is crucial that congregations give patient, thoughtful, and loving attention to promoting intergenerational worship practices that allow each generation to benefit from the strengths of each other and to complement each others' weaknesses.

Importantly, making worship more child-accessible does not mean making it childish. To the contrary, challenging members of all ages to grow in understanding, in biblically shaped affection, in faithful reception of the Word of God, in faithful prayer, and in faithful participation in the sacraments most often involves running away from all that is merely sentimental, childish, or simplistic.

The agenda here in Danny Hyde's book is nothing less than full-orbed discipleship to Jesus Christ shaped in intergenerational community, all conducted with graced awareness of how the Holy Spirit is forming us to grow up into our full stature as sons and daughters of God. May the Holy Spirit use this book to equip families and congregations to that end.

John D. Witvliet

Calvin Institute of Christian Worship

Calvin College and Calvin Theological Seminary

Grand Rapids, Michigan

Acknowledgments

FIRST AND FOREMOST, I would like to acknowledge the generations of godly saints at Escondido Christian / United Reformed Church who unassumingly taught me the principles in this book by their example. The intergenerational assembly of grandparents, parents, children, and grandchildren who participated in worship week in and week out was such a blessing to behold while I was still a newly Reformed seminary student from 1997–2000. To my brothers and sisters at the Oceanside United Reformed Church I offer the encouragement that I see how you accept children into your midst every Lord's Day. It's often loud—causing me to preach even louder!—but the sacrifices so many of you are making to raise your children with you in public worship will not be in vain. The Holy Spirit will use you as an example for generations to come!

I thank those who assisted me to make this a more readable and understandable book. Dr. Mark Jones, pastor of Faith Presbyterian Church (PCA) in Vancouver, British Columbia, was a tremendous encouragement in the writing of this book. Not only his editorial comments but also our phone conversations about this topic have kept me motivated to write this book as a service to the church. Anna Phillips and Caitlin Lloyd also offered wonderful editorial assistance. Tim Challies and I dialoged as I wrote this book, helping me draw some helpful distinctions to make this book useable to a wider community of Christian parents. John and

Acknowledgments

Debby Rau were my final set of eyes in reading and editing prior to publication.

Finally, I must thank above all my dear wife, Karajean, of whom I cannot say enough. You have modeled everything in this book and then some, week after week, year after year, first with one energetic boy, then a second, then a third, and now with a girl added to the mix! You are the Proverbs 31 women *par excellence*:

> Her children rise up and call her blessed;
>
> Her husband also, and he praises her:
>
> "Many women have done excellently,
>
> But you surpass them all." (Prov 31:28–29)

Abbreviations

BC   Belgic Confession

CD   Canons of Dort

HC   Heidelberg Catechism

WCF   Westminster Confession of Faith

WLC   Westminster Larger Catechism

WSC   Westminster Shorter Catechism

Introduction

As YOU ENTER THE sanctuary, you notice them. Then, taking your seat next to a family, they are right there. Throughout the ensuing service, you see them—and especially *hear* them. Not only are they in the service, but they also fill its air with their unmistakable "joyful noise" (Ps 100:1 KJV)—and I emphasize *noise*. But the Bible says this is a good thing: "Out of the mouth of babes and nursing infants you have ordained strength" (Ps 8:2), that is, the strength ascribed to God in praise (Matt 21:16).[1]

One of the things that strikes visitors to the congregation I serve is that unlike so many churches around us, our worship is filled with the presence of children—lots of them.[2] Their presence in public worship is not only striking, but also strange, since if those who visit us have any church background at all, they have never seen children in worship. I know it was striking and strange for me so many years ago as it may be for you. In fact, the idea of *your* children sitting or standing next to you during congregational prayer, singing, or the pastor's sermon is downright scary.

1. The Greek translation of the Old Testament, known as the Septuagint (LXX), translates this as "Out of the mouth of babes and sucklings hast thou perfected *praise*." In Matthew 21:16 Jesus follows this translation.

2. For an introduction to what a Reformed church is all about, see Hyde, *Welcome to a Reformed Church*. For a specific introduction to Reformed worship, see Hyde, *What to Expect in Reformed Worship*.

This is why I am writing this book. I want to take away that strangeness and scariness of having children in worship. In the place of these feelings I want to make a case for the benefit and blessing of this practice because public worship is the nursery of the Holy Spirit. Before I do that, let me lay out some basic premises of what follows.

In writing this book I am assuming two audiences. First, I am writing to those of you who worship in a church that encourages and welcomes little ones to join with the rest of the congregation. I know it is exhausting and often exasperating. I want to offer you some encouragement to continue on this path. Second, I am writing to those of you who may only know the Sunday School / children's church model of ministry, in which children do not participate in part of or the whole of congregational worship, but instead have their own age-specific class, ministry, or service. Perhaps you are a member, on a worship committee, or are a pastor in such a church. Perhaps you have recently begun worshipping in a Reformed church. I want to encourage you to consider the benefits of including children in your weekly services.

In writing this book I have two purposes. First, I want to make a case that welcoming children in worship is a practice consistent with the examples we see in Scripture and is a highly beneficial practice because it places our little ones in the nursery of the Holy Spirit—public worship. Public worship being the nursery of the Holy Spirit is an image of ancient vintage. The ancient bishop of Carthage Cyprian (200–258) once wrote, "You cannot have God for your father unless you have the Church for your mother."[3] This image of the church as a mother with children was approvingly adopted by the Reformation pastors and theologians of the sixteenth century such as John Calvin (1509–1564): "The church, into whose bosom God is pleased to gather his sons, not only that they may be nourished by her help and ministry as long as they are infants and children, but also that they may be guided by her motherly care until they mature and at last reach the goal of faith."[4]

3. Cyprian, "Unity of the Catholic Church," 127–28.

4. Calvin, *Institutes*, 4.1.1.

If the church is the Christian's mother, then public worship is her nursery. My second purpose is to offer some practical advice on how you can bring children into worship and help them make the most of their time worshipping alongside of you.

Let me also offer two caveats so that you know where I am going with all of this, but also where I am not going. First, I am writing out of the conviction that the following classic distinction is valid and helpful with this practice: including children in worship is of the wellbeing (*bene esse*) of the church and not of the essence (*esse*) of the church. I believe it is the best practice, but I cannot say it must be the only practice. In other words, in churches that have their roots in the Reformed, Presbyterian, Congregational, and Baptist families of churches, true churches are those that have three clear marks: pure preaching of the gospel, pure administration of the sacraments (or, ordinances), and the practice of church discipline (e.g., BC, art. 29). This is important to guard us from adding the practice of children in worship as a fourth mark of the church, as some in their over-zealousness might do. Second, I am also writing out of the firm conviction that the local church is the hub of Christian spirituality. This means that members are to be in submission to their pastors and elders (e.g., Heb 13:17) and that pastors are to shepherd their flocks with love and patience (1 Pet 5:1–5). Too often people can be pitted against their pastors by over-zealous adherence to secondary issues, such as the topic of this book. If you are a member of a church that does not have children in its worship, and if you think this is a good idea, then I exhort you to work together with your pastors and elders. Have a conversation with them and let the Lord work through the ordinary means of church life and government in your church. Do not divide your church. Show love, patience, humility, and deference to those over you in the Lord, just like they must show it to you as shepherds to sheep.

All this to say that my prayer for us all is that we would wrestle with the question of how can we best nurture our children unto faith and salvation in Christ as local bodies of believers. We can do this together, as those who follow our forefathers' zeal for their little ones:

> Let children hear the mighty deeds
> Which God performed of old,
> Which in our younger years we saw
> And which our fathers told.
> He bids us make His glories known,
> The works of power and grace,
> That we convey His wonders down
> Through every rising race.

> Our lips shall tell them to our sons,
> And they again to theirs;
> And generations yet unborn
> Must teach them to their heirs;
> Thus shall they learn, in God alone
> Their hope securely stands;
> That they may not forget His works,
> But honor His commands.[5]

5. CRC, *Psalter Hymnal* (1976), #150; OPC, *Trinity Hymnal*, #364.

1

Children's Church or Children of the Church?

WHETHER WE REALIZE IT, American evangelical[1] Christian churches exist well after the rise of the Sunday school movement (ca. 1880) and developmental psychology. While not wrong in and of themselves, these ideas have affected how churches approach children and how we as Bible-believing Christians approach them as well. As R. C. Sproul has taught so many of us, ideas have consequences.[2] Robert Raikes (1735–1811) began the Sunday school movement in Gloucester, England, as a means of social outreach to poor children. It quickly became a means of evangelizing children of non-Christian parents.[3] To do this these children were taught outside of public church services. This commendable model of evangelizing the children *outside* the church eventually became the model of educating the children *inside* the church, yet outside

---

1. I recognize the fluidity of language and the problems that have been associated with the meaning of the term "evangelicalism" in our time. I am using it in its historic sense of those who believed the gospel in the sixteenth-century Protestant Reformation.

2. Sproul, *Consequences of Ideas.*

3. See Power, *Rise and Progress of Sunday Schools.*

the body of the church in groups deemed to be "age-appropriate" by developmental psychology.

Our Age

Mixed with a healthy dose of developmental psychology, the Sunday school and children's church phenomena changed Christians' thoughts about the place of children in the church from liturgical (worshipping) terms into educational terms.[4] Well-known Old Testament scholar Walter Brueggemann has described the situation like this: "Church education has been intensely interested in the social sciences and has indeed learned much from them . . . But in the midst of attention to the social sciences, I suggest that the biblical, theological disciplines have not been a full partner."[5] The result can be seen in churches that offer things such as "children's church," often described with cute verbiage like "Wee Worship," "Little Lambs," or "K.I.T." (Kids in Training) for the littlest children, or hip terms to express how extreme and cutting-edge the youth ministry is for junior high and high school students. As an example, an online search revealed how two typical evangelical churches, Calvary Chapel in Boston and Calvary Chapel in Baltimore, explain the place of children on a typical Sunday morning:

> Sunday School (during morning service)
> The Sunday School program focuses on using the Word of God to build a strong foundation in the lives of the children and foster worship of the Lord from their hearts. Sunday School starts with a time of worship where the children are encouraged to praise the Lord in voice and dance. From there the children, ages 4–12, are separated into several classes where they are taught the Word.[6]
> While you're attending our services, we provide fun activities, Bible teaching and children's worship for your

4. Clark, "Children and Worship," 161–62.

5. Brueggemann, *Creative Word*, 2.

6. Calvary Chapel in the City (Boston), http://calvarychapelinthecity.com/#/kids-youth/childrens-church-4-12.

kids, no matter what their ages. From the nursery all the way through middle school, your kids will be ministered to on their own level, in a way they can relate to and enjoy!⁷

As was stated above, the rationale behind children's church at any level is not explicitly based on biblical teaching of worship and the place of children in worship, but educational: children are incapable of understanding and need to hear the Word at their level. Another pragmatic reason often given is that the absence of children in the worship service, especially during the sermon, helps the adults to "get something out of the sermon," which they otherwise would not if they were "distracted" by children. This is the spirit of the age (*zeitgeist*) in which we live. Consider an on-line review by a visitor to the aforementioned Calvary Chapel in Baltimore:

> We sat down in the service and during worship one of the ushers (at least I think he was) came up to me and asked if I was going to put Delilah and James in their "class." When I said no, he told me that they really needed to go because they really try to teach the kids "on their level." He then said that kids really weren't supposed to be in the sanctuary. I told him if it were a problem that we wouldn't come back. Guy says "Okay." He walked away. During the break in worship where you're supposed to go greet people, usher guy came back over to me. He told me that children under seven definitely weren't allowed in the sanctuary and that I would have to take them to the nursery. I said that I wasn't leaving them with people I didn't know, and he said I could stay in the nursery with them. (They weren't making noise or being disruptive). I told dh [the reviewer's husband] that I wasn't going to go to church there and he decided that we would just leave then.⁸

7. Calvary Chapel (Baltimore), http://www.calvarychapelbaltimore.org/ministries/childrens-ministry.

8. Elizabeth B., online review of Calvary Chapel (Rosedale, MD), *Insider-Pages*, November 6, 2010, http://www.insiderpages.com/b/3715904264.

Thankfully in our day, there are those within evangelical churches who recognize that we need to reevaluate such an approach to public worship. One example of this is Harold Best, former dean of the Conservatory of Music at Wheaton College. In his book *Unceasing Worship*, he wrote a scathing rebuke of the practice of dividing the church:

> To divide congregations into age groups, style groups and preference groups is to be semi- or even pseudo-corporate. The body of Christ is as chronologically and stylistically whole as it is spiritually whole. It is ironic—worse, scripturally troublesome—to see local assemblies broken into groups, each doing their niche worship, for that is all it really seems to be. It is disheartening to think that church leadership has so succumbed to the secondary things about corporate gatherings that it feels constrained to go in this direction.[9]

Even the *Wall Street Journal* recently published an article about Laura Vanderkam's experience of having her child ushered out of a service because of noise concerns and her subsequent investigation into the attitudes of churches toward children. Her research revealed that "this turns out to be a major topic of discussion in a growing number of churches," and that churches' attitudes toward children are beginning to reflect historic Christian practice and not merely pragmatic approaches of Sunday school and other methods.[10] The article chronicled the words of another mother, Kate Wicker, an Atlanta mom of a four-year-old, two-year-old, and a baby, who attends a Roman Catholic Church: "How can we baptize children, welcoming them to the body of Christ, and then say 'until you're old enough to not make any noise and sit still you're not welcome here?'" In fact, this mother even cited Pope Benedict XVI, who said of the Mass, "For this reason parents are called to make their children discover the value and importance of

---

9. Best, *Unceasing Worship*, 74.

10. Laura Vanderkam, "Seen and Not Heard in Church," *Wall Street Journal*, December 4, 2009, http://online.wsj.com/article/SB10001424052748704335904574495761234081316.html.

the response to Christ's invitation, who calls the whole Christian family to Sunday Mass."[11] Along with my theological tradition, I believe the Mass is a serious theological error (HC, Q&A 80); yet, Benedict XVI expressed what has been the historic understanding of all Christian churches in including the children of the church in the worship of the church.[12]

A Historic Practice

As a pastor of a church that whole-heartedly welcomes children into its services, reviews like those above in which parents with children are excluded from worship break my heart on so many levels, least of which is the fact that churches that do such a thing usually pride themselves on having "no creed but Christ" and following no book but the Bible. But, if we as the heirs of the Protestant Reformation doctrine of *sola Scriptura*—that "Scripture alone [is] the primary and absolute norm of doctrine"[13]—we then need not only to affirm it but to seek to apply it as best we can in all areas of faith, life, and worship.

Christian churches have deep historic roots. We need to recognize this and wrestle with how our practices may or may not reflect classic practice.[14] For example, we read of intergenerational

11. Benedict XVI, "On Importance of Sunday Mass," *Catholic Online*, June 13, 2005 (translation of address given June 12, 2005, from pope's window, St. Peter's Square), http://www.catholic.org/featured/headline.php?ID=2258.

12. For a popular explanation of this question and answer, see Venema, "Lord's Supper," *Outlook*. For a more scholarly explanation, see Venema, "Lord's Supper," *Mid-America Journal of Theology*.

13. Muller, *Dictionary of Latin and Greek*, 284.

14. In the words of Richard Muller, the relationship between *sola Scriptura* and church history is expressed this way:

> Finally, it ought to be noted that *sola Scriptura* was never meant as a denial of the usefulness of the Christian tradition as a subordinate norm in theology. The views of the Reformers developed out of a debate in the late medieval theology over the relation of Scripture and tradition, one party viewing the two as coequal norms, the other party viewing Scripture as the absolute and therefore prior norm, but allowing tradition a derivative but important secondary role in doctrinal

worship in the *Apostolic Constitutions*, a fourth-century document of church government and guidelines from Syria. It spoke of the assembling of the church for worship, with one of the duties of the deacons to arrange the place of each member of the congregation. It describes the first half of the service, known as the liturgy of the Word. There were two Old Testament readings, Psalms were sung, then there were New Testament readings from Acts, the Epistles, and finally, the Gospels. After the readings, the presbyters and the bishop exhorted the congregation. Before describing the second half of the service, known as the liturgy of the Eucharist, the *Apostolic Constitutions* describes the duties of the deacons in arranging the place of each member of the congregation. In addition to the division of clergy and laity and of men and women, we read:

> For as the shepherds place all the brute creatures distinctly, I mean goats and sheep, according to their kind and age, and still every one runs together, like to his like; so is it to be in the Church. Let the young persons sit by themselves, if there be a place for them; if not, let them stand upright. But let those that are already stricken in years sit in order. For the children which stand, let their fathers and mothers take them to them. Let the younger women also sit by themselves, if there be a place for them; but if there be not, let them stand behind the women. Let those women which are married, and have children, be placed by themselves . . . and let the deacon be the disposer of the places, that every one of those that comes in may go to his proper place, and may not sit at the entrance. In like manner, let the deacon oversee the people, that nobody may whisper, nor slumber, nor laugh, nor nod; for all ought in the church to stand wisely, and soberly, and

---

statement. The Reformers and the Protestant orthodox held the latter view, on the assumption that tradition was a useful guide, that the trinitarian and christological statements of Nicaea, Constantinople, and Chalcedon were expressions of biblical truth, and that the great teachers of the church provided valuable instruction in theology that always needed to be evaluated in the light of Scripture.

Muller, *Dictionary of Latin and Greek*, 284. See also the collection of essays in Kistler, *Sola Scriptura*.

attentively, having their attention fixed upon the word of
the Lord (2.7.57).[15]

To be clear, I am not arguing that just because something was
done in the past that we should necessarily do it precisely as it
was then, in the present. What I am saying is that exposing our
practices to those of earlier generations helps us to evaluate and be
ever-reforming (*semper reformanda*) of our practice according to
the Word of God.

The Place of Children in the Church

As a Reformed pastor I firmly believe that the Scriptures teach that
children of believing parents are members of the visible church.[16]
In Reformed theological terms, they are members of the new
covenant's administration of the one covenant of grace.[17] Let me
explain briefly.

What is a covenant? It can be variously described as God's
solemn promise, his oath, or his bond that is put into effect with
some outward ceremony. For example, in marriage, promises and
vows are made, and then rings are exchanged to symbolize those
promises.[18]

God's promise to be gracious toward sinners has been revealed to his people from creation to the new creation in the form
of covenants. After Adam sinned (Gen 3:1–7; Rom 5:12–19),
God found him and Eve hiding behind the trees and their own

---

15. "Constitutions of the Holy Apostles," 421.

16. See Hyde, *Jesus Loves the Little Children*, 37–43.

17. On the covenant of grace, see Bullinger, *Brief Exposition*; Hendriksen,
Covenant of Grace; Horton, *God of Promise*.

18. The primary author of the Heidelberg Catechism, Zacharius Ursinus
(1534–83), defined a covenant as "a mutual contract, or agreement between
two parties, in which the one party binds itself to the other to accomplish
something upon certain conditions, giving or receiving something, which
is accompanied with certain outward signs and symbols, for the purpose of
ratifying in the most solemn manner the contract entered into, and for the
sake of confirming it, that the engagement may be kept inviolate." Ursinus,
Commentary, 97.

garments of fig leaves (Gen 3:8–9). Amidst his words of judgment (Gen 3:14–19), he also preached the gospel of a coming salvation: "And I will put enmity between you and the woman, and between your seed and her Seed; He shall bruise your head, and you shall bruise His heel" (Gen 3:15; John 12:31; Rom 16:20; Rev 12). He even signified and sealed that gospel promise by his actions, sacrificing animals to make coverings for them (Gen 3:21).

God progressively revealed more about this to Noah (Gen 9:9–17), Abraham (Gen 15; 17), Israel (Exod 19–24), David (2 Sam 7), and exiled Israel (Jer 31:31–34). In this unfolding of his covenant, God promised more and more of who the Savior was to come. To Eve the Lord simply promised a seed (Gen 3:15), to Abraham a son (Gen 15:4), to Judah that he would come from his line (Gen 49:10), to David that he would be of his house (2 Sam 7:13–14), to the prophets that his mother would be a virgin (Isa 7:14), that he would be born in Bethlehem (Mic 5:2), that he would be born after the captivity in Babylon (Dan 9:24–27), that he would suffer, and then be glorified (Isa 53), and that he would have a prophetic forerunner (Mal 3:1). All these gracious promises were fulfilled in Jesus Christ (Luke 3:22; Heb 9:14–28) and will be culminated in the new heavens and new earth (Rev 21:1–6; 22:1–5). All these are what the Paul calls "the covenants of promise" (Eph 2:12), that is, that from its beginning to its end, the Bible is a story about one God, one Savior, one salvation, and one people. In theological terms, there is one "covenant of grace."[19] In the words of the Westminster Confession of Faith,

> This covenant was differently administered in the time of the law, and in the time of the Gospel: under the law it was administered by promises, prophecies, sacrifices, circumcision, the paschal lamb, and other types and ordinances delivered to the people of the Jews, all foresignifying Christ to come; which were, for that time,

19. The Heidelberg Catechism summarizes the great history of God's covenant of grace mentioned above by saying that the gospel was "first revealed in Paradise, afterwards proclaimed by the holy Patriarchs and Prophets, and foreshadowed by the sacrifices and other ceremonies of the law, and finally fulfilled by his well-beloved Son" (Q&A 19).

sufficient and efficacious, through the operation of the Spirit, to instruct and build up the elect in faith in the promised Messiah, by whom they had full remission of sins, and eternal salvation; and is called the Old Testament. (WCF, 7.5)

Under the Gospel, when Christ, the substance, was exhibited, the ordinances in which this covenant is dispensed are the preaching of the Word, and the administration of the sacraments of Baptism and the Lord's Supper: which, though fewer in number, and administered with more simplicity, and less outward glory, yet, in them, it is held forth in more fullness, evidence, and spiritual efficacy, to all nations, both Jews and Gentiles; and is called the New Testament. There are not therefore two covenants of grace, differing in substance, but one and the same, under various dispensations. (WCF, 7.6)

With whom does God make his covenant? From the point of view of God and eternity, he made it with Christ and the elect. As the Westminster Larger Catechism (1647) says, "The covenant of grace was made with Christ as the second Adam, and in him with all the elect as his seed" (Q&A 31).[20] From our point of view in history, God made his covenant with believers and their children. The Canons of Dort (1618–19) express this perspective when they say, "The children of believers are holy, not by nature, but in virtue of the covenant of grace (*sed beneficio foederis gratuiti*), in which they together with the parents are comprehended" (1.17).[21]

The Old Testament teaches this. For example, in the book of Genesis the covenant line was continued through Adam's son Seth, not Cain (Gen 4:25; 5:3); through Noah's son Shem, not Ham or Japheth (Gen 9:9; 11:10–26); through Terah's son Abram, not Nahor, Haran, or Haran's son, Lot (Gen 11:27—12:1; ch. 13); through Abraham's son Isaac, not Ishamel (Gen 17); and through Isaac's

20. On this question and answer, see the lengthy exposition of Ridgley, *Body Of Divinity*, 2:167–85.

21. For a popular treatment of this article, see Pronk, *Expository Sermons*, 89–99. For academic works, see de Boer, "O, Ye Women," 261–90; Venema, "Election and Salvation."

son Jacob, not Esau (Gen 25:19—26:5). Eve's "seed" (plural) would crush the serpent's head (Gen 3:15). With Noah *and his family* the Lord made his covenant (Gen 9:9). When God called Abraham he said, "And I will establish My covenant between Me and you and your descendants after you in their generations, for an everlasting covenant, to be God to you and your descendants after you" (Gen 17:7). In the Ten Commandments, the Lord threatened his curse for disobedience and his blessings for obedience "upon the children to the third and fourth generations of those who hate Me, but showing mercy to thousands, to those who love Me and keep My commandments" (Exod 20:5–6), because of covenantal connection between fathers and sons.

The New Testament teaches this. The New Testament never says that the relationship of believers' children to the covenant community has changed. Neither Jesus nor the apostles revoke this teaching that children of professing believers belong to the covenant people of God. They do not say our children are to be treated differently in the New Testament from the way they were in the Old. Instead, the children of believers are "covenant children" in the attitude of the Lord Jesus himself (Matt 19:14, cf. 18:1–6; Mark 10:14–16; Luke 18:15–17). We read of the promise of the Lord's grace at the beginning of the new covenant in Acts 2:39: "For the promise is to you and to your children, and to all who are afar off, as many as the Lord our God will call." We see this idea of children belonging to Christ's family and receiving its blessings in the writings of Apostle Paul, where he gives pastoral instruction on the responsibility of children to their parents, citing the fifth commandment, and their parents' responsibility to raise them as members of the Christian church, to "bring them up in the training and admonition of the Lord" (Eph 6:4; Col 3:20). Paul says the same in 1 Corinthians 7:14, speaking to the issue of mixed marriages between a believer and an unbeliever, saying, "For the unbelieving husband is sanctified by the wife, and the unbelieving wife is sanctified by the husband; otherwise your children would be unclean, but now they are holy." The family unit is "sanctified" even if only the husband or the wife is a believer. This is not "sanctification" or "holiness" as he normally speaks, in the sense of the ongoing life of becoming more and more conformed to the image of Jesus Christ (e.g., Rom 8:29), but in a typically Old Testament sense, that even these broken, divided families are still a part of the larger people of God.

Our children belonging to the covenant of grace and receiving the blessings of it is like belonging to a family. As members of a family, everyone from the oldest to the youngest receives the blessings of the family such as love, shelter, and guidance. We do not regard our children as outside our family any more than we should regard them as outside God's family, the church. As one writer stated, why would the Apostle Paul go out of his way to address the children of the congregations in Ephesus and Colossae if they were not a part of the covenant of grace?[22]

The historic Reformed catechisms and confessions also teach that children of believers belong to the administration of the covenant of grace. The Westminster Confession says, "The visible church . . . consists of all these throughout the world that profess the true religion, together with their children (WCF, 25.2). The Westminster Larger Catechism explains that "the visible church is a society made up of all such as in all ages and places of the world do profess the true religion, and of their children" (WLC, Q&A 62). Because of this, it goes on to say that "infants descending from parents, either both or but one of them professing faith in Christ, and obedience to him, are, in that respect, within the covenant, and to be baptized" (WLC, Q&A 166). In the words of the Heidelberg Catechism, infants "as well as their parents, belong to the covenant and people of God" and therefore are "by Baptism, as a sign of the covenant, to be ingrafted into the Christian Church, and distinguished from the children of unbelievers, as was done in the Old Testament by Circumcision, in place of which in the New Testament Baptism is appointed" (HC, Q&A 74).

While you may not have this same theological understanding, experientially we most likely view our children the same way. And we can work together from this starting point. For example, have

22. Bosma, *Exposition of Reformed Doctrine*, 266.

you ever sung "Jesus Loves the Little Children" or "Jesus Loves Me" with your children before they go to bed? Do you pray with them at meals and before you tuck them into bed at night? Maybe you even had your child "dedicated" in a public service at your church. If so, what did you promise to do? You promised to raise your child in a Christian way as part of a Christian home. You may even have sung words such as these:

> The fruit of love, this gift of life,
>
> we place, O God, within your care.
>
> To know your grace and guiding hand
>
> in years to come is now our prayer.
>
> With humble joy we recognize
>
> a task that only has begun.
>
> A sacred charge lies in our arms
>
> to cradle faith and pass it on.[23]

What is the purpose of doing these things with your children? You do so because there is an inherent understanding in all of us that our children are different from the children of the world and that we are to raise them differently.[24] As the Belgic Confession teaches, by baptism "we are received into the Church of God, and separated from all other people and strange religions, that we may wholly belong to Him whose ensign and banner we bear" (BC, art. 34).[25]

The reason for this is that throughout the Scriptures we learn that the children of the church are distinguished from the children of the world. In saying this, let me be absolutely clear about something you may be thinking. I am not saying that all the children

23. From "The Fruit of Love," in *Worship & Rejoice* (hymnal), 682.

24. Hyde, *Jesus Loves the Little Children*, 37.

25. See also the Second Helvetic Confession (1561/66), art. 20. For an explanation of this, see Ursinus, *Commentary on the Heidelberg Catechism*, 365–76; Bastingius, *Exposition*, 100, column 1–102, column 1.

of the church necessarily are or even will be regenerated, justified, and saved. In fact, the Reformed forefathers were crystal clear that there is a difference between our children being "in the church" merely externally and being "of [the church]" internally (BC, art. 29).[26] In the words of the Apostle Paul, "For they are not all Israel, who are of Israel" (Rom 9:6). While children are in the church with their parents it is only by faith alone in Christ alone that they receive the benefits of Christ.

It is vital for us to keep these distinctions clear, or else we will either overestimate our children's relationship to Christ and his church (and presume they are all elect) or underestimate their relationship (and believe there is no benefit to their being in the church with us).[27] One balanced approach was offered in the seventeenth century by the Dutch pastor, Jacobus Koelman. While I realize his advice may not be applicable to all who read this book, since not all baptize their children, nevertheless the spirit of what he says applies to all of us as parents:

> Do not be satisfied with the external baptism administered in the church but continue to occupy yourself with baptism through your prayers and by the renewal of the solemn promises made before the Lord and his church at the time of baptism. . . . Pray that he may forgive them and by his Spirit unite them with him in Christ Jesus and fulfill and confirm his own institution of baptism. Pray that he may regenerate them, that he may kill, crucify, and subdue the old Adam, the corrupt nature they have received from you. Pray that he may cleanse them and renew them after his image in knowledge, righteousness, and holiness, that he may strengthen them by his grace so that as they grow up they may resist and overcome the world, the flesh, and the devil and serve the Lord in newness of life and the comfort of the Holy Spirit all the days of their lives.[28]

---

26. CRC, *Psalter Hymnal* (1988), 847.
27. On this, see Beeke, *Bringing the Gospel to Covenant Children*, 3–11.
28. Koelman, *Duties of Parents*, 41.

> ... Do not believe unconditionally that all your chil-
> dren are beloved by God and will certainly inherit salva-
> tion or that they are truly sanctified in Christ and already
> born again and in a blessed state, for that is unknown
> and uncertain. ... You must therefore pray for them and
> instruct them in the faith and in the Word. You must
> bring them up in all godliness so that they themselves in
> their own person may consent to that covenant with God
> and surrender themselves to it in order to be saved.[29]

Since our children belong to us as believers they have a relationship to the church because of us, they are different. Because
they are different we must pray for them. We must instruct them in
the teaching of the Word. We must model for them a life in the way
of the Lord. We must include them in the worship of the church to
which they belong.

Children-Friendly Churches

With a renewal of biblical doctrine in many evangelical circles
today, for example, among "New Calvinism,"[30] it is a great time
to reevaluate our practice and to ask how we can become more
"children-friendly" as churches in the area of worship. This is also
a great time to do this given the content in which we live, as our
children are being assaulted in their faith more than ever before.
Even before many children are born they are assaulted by "Pro
Choice." Our culture more and more is seeking to allure children
into a worldview of hedonism, materialism, and narcissism. The
church, therefore, needs to be a refuge for children from the earliest of age. One practical expression of this is in welcoming our
children to join us before the throne of God's grace in worship,
giving them a meaningful place in the church.[31] As the church
education professor, John Westerhoff III, has shown, the biblical example of three generations in the church's worship results

29. Ibid., 42.
30. Van Biema, "New Calvinism."
31. Sandell, *Including Children in Worship*, 7.

in interaction and sharing among generations as well as a sense of experiencing the whole community of faith.[32] The children of believers, therefore, are children of the church and belong in the Holy Spirit's most child-friendly nursery—public worship.

32. Westerhoff III, *Will Our Children Have Faith?*, 53–54. Cf. Bacon, *Revealed to Babes*; Ward, *Worship Is for Kids*.

2

Children in Worship in Scripture

THE PRACTICE OF CHILDREN joining their parents and the rest of the congregation in worship is consistent with what we see in Scripture. To reiterate what I said in the introduction, there is a distinction between things prescribed in the Word of God and things described in the Word of God. While there is no "thus saith the Lord" concerning children in worship, there are various descriptions of children among the people of God in worship in both Testaments. Liturgical scholars have described this in terms of an assumption on the basis of the covenant idea that is so pervasive in the Old Testament. Children among Israel's worship was a basic assumption and not a self-consciously explained practice.[1] Recently Jeremy Walker summarized this position in the following way:

> The constant presumption of Scripture is that children were present in the worship of the people of God. In Nehemiah's time, men and women and all those who could hear with understanding gathered to hear Ezra the scribe read the Law (Neh 8.1–3; Ezra 10.1). Moses certainly anticipated the literal "children" of Israel to be present when the Law was read (Deut 31.12–13). Paul's letters, intended to be read to the churches, assume the intelligent presence of children (Eph 6.1–4; Col 3.20),

1. Clark, "Children and Worship," 161.

and children were present when the Lord Jesus taught
(Matt 18.1–5; 19.13–15).[2]

What I want to do in this chapter, then, is to draw out of several examples from the Old and New Testaments in which children were in the presence of the worshipping community, to show you that this is a practice worthy of your discussion, consideration, and implementation.

Old Testament

Besides what we saw above with God working through the covenantal structure of the family line in the Old Testament, toward the end of the Old Testament the prophets foresaw the dawn of the new covenant era, in which children had a significant place. Isaiah prophesied a day in which "all your children shall be taught by the Lord, and great shall be the peace of your children" (Isa 54:13). He also said that in those days, all the nations would be drawn to God's people because the Lord himself would be in their midst:

Arise, shine;

For your light has come!

And the glory of the Lord is risen upon you.

For behold, the darkness shall cover the earth,

And deep darkness the people;

But the Lord will arise over you,

And His glory will be seen upon you.

The Gentiles shall come to your light,

And kings to the brightness of your rising.

Lift up your eyes all around, and see:

They all gather together, they come to you;

Your sons shall come from afar,

And your daughters shall be nursed at your side.
(Isa 60:1–4)

2. Walker, "Attendance of Children in Public Worship."

Among the Gentiles converted to the faith of Israel would be their sons and daughters, whom Isaiah says would be "nursed at your side."[3] Matthew Henry applied this to the issue of children and worship when he said, "The church's children must be nursed at her side, not sent out to be nursed among strangers." Why did he apply this passage this way? Because "there, where alone the unadulterated milk of the word is to be had, must the church's newborn babes be nursed, *that they may grow thereby*, 1 Pet. ii.1, 2."[4]

Another prophet, Zechariah, envisioned the new covenant as a day to come in which the place of children among the people of God were described in a very touching image: "The streets of the city shall be full of boys and girls playing in its streets" (Zech 8:5). Is there any better way to show their place among God's people than their doing what they love the most—playing?[5]

When it comes to those children being a part of public worship, there are several examples from various high points in the life of Israel.

The Exodus

The Lord stated his great purpose in his dealings with Pharaoh in the book of Exodus when he said: "Thus says the Lord, 'Israel is My son, My firstborn. So I say to you, let My son go that he may serve Me'" (Exod 4:22–23). The Lord's purpose in redeeming his "son" was that his "son" would worship him. As the drama continues between Pharaoh and Moses, we read of Moses saying, "Thus says the Lord, the God of Israel, 'Let My people go, that they may hold a feast to Me in the wilderness'" (Exod 5:1). And in Exodus 7:16 the Lord spoke again of the purpose for this deliverance: "that they may serve Me in the wilderness." Later, in the actual narrative of the ten plagues upon Egypt (Exod 7–12), we read a fascinating

3. The ESV and NIV translate this as "carried on the hip." See the comments of Young, *Book of Isaiah*, 446.

4. Henry, *Commentary*, 1201.

5. For a children's address on this passage, see Ryle, *Boys and Girls Playing*, 1–9.

dialog between Moses and Aaron on the one hand and Pharaoh on the other about who would go into the wilderness and worship the Lord:

> Then Pharaoh's servants said to him, "How long shall this man be a snare to us? Let the men go, that they may serve the Lord their God. Do you not yet know that Egypt is destroyed?" So Moses and Aaron were brought again to Pharaoh, and he said to them, "Go, serve the Lord your God. Who are the ones that are going?" And Moses said, "We will go with our *young* and our old; with our *sons* and *daughters*, with our flocks and our herds we will go, for we must hold a feast to the Lord." Then he said to them, "The Lord had better be with you when I let you and your *little ones* go! Beware, for evil is ahead of you." (Exod 10:7–10, emphasis added)

As Moses said, all Israel was to go into the wilderness to celebrate the feast of the Lord, including the young (*na'ar*) sons and daughters, which is a word that can be used to describe a child from infancy as with Moses (Exod 2:6), a weaned child as with Samuel (1 Sam 1:23, 25, 27), an older boy such as Ishmael (Gen 21:12), or a teenager like Joseph (Gen 37:2). Those whom the Lord called his "son" and "people," Moses defines as "our young and our old . . . our sons and daughters" (Exod 10:9). All those from the least to the greatest were the people the Lord desired to worship him. Yet Pharaoh would not agree to this, saying that their "little ones" (*taphchem*) could not go along (Exod 10:10).

The controversy between Moses and Pharaoh went from Pharaoh refusing to let them go (Exod 5:2), to Pharaoh allowing them to go but not very far (Exod 8:28), to allowing them to go but without their children (Exod 10:10–11). The great Puritan commentator, Matthew Henry (1662–1714), commented on this text with a relevant application; for behind Pharaoh was Satan, who "does all he can to hinder those that serve God themselves from bringing their children in to serve him." Why has Satan been so concerned in the history of God's people to try keeping their children out of the Lord's assemblies? "He is a sworn enemy to early piety, knowing how destructive it is to the interests of his kingdom; whatever would hinder us from engaging our children to the utmost in God's service, we have reason to suspect the hand of Satan in it."[6] These are weighty words for us to meditate upon.

Passover

As the people later prepared for the exodus from Egypt, they were given regulations for the celebration of the Passover feast:

> And it shall be, when your children [*beneychem*] say to you, "What do you mean by this service?" that you shall say, "It is the Passover sacrifice of the Lord, who passed over the houses of the children [*beney*] of Israel in Egypt when He struck the Egyptians and delivered our households." (Exod 12:26–27)

Admittedly, the Passover meal could be considered what we call family worship, as each family or group of families gathered in a home for this service. Yet, since all Israel celebrated the Passover that night, it was a corporate festival of worship. And the Lord wanted to ensure that the children had a vital role in its liturgy (order of service). Jewish custom is that the youngest child in the household asks the questions at the Passover meal, which in turn prompts an explanation by the father.[7]

According to the Passover narrative, the practical and blessed benefit of Israel's children in the worship of the Lord was that it led them to ask questions. Further, it was not enough for Israelite adults to know that they were to have an annual feast, but they had to know the reasons for the feast. Theology that does not become biography is wishful thinking. As Matthew Poole commented, "God expects this even from the Jewish children, and much more from Christian men, that they should inquire and understand

6. Henry, *Commentary*, 108.

7. Gispen, *Exodus*, 124. Matthew Henry said of this text, "It is a good thing to see children inquisitive about the things of God; it is to be hoped that those who are careful to ask for the way will find it. Christ himself, when a child, *heard and asked questions*, Luke ii.46." Henry, *Commentary*, 111.

what is said or done in the public worship or service of God."[8] In other words, Poole said this applies to Christian parents as they talk to their children before, during, and after they have worshipped together. Because it is the child who asks the questions, this means that the parents have to be equipped with the answer.[9] The catechizing (oral instruction by way of questions and answers) that resulted from worship is inherently experiential.[10]

After Israel left Egypt in the exodus, Moses spoke to the people about the Passover as well as the ceremony of consecrating the firstborn. When these ceremonies were performed, children were among the participants. As with chapter 12, the children would ask questions because of their presence in worship:

> And you shall tell your son [*le-bincha*] in that day, saying, "This is done because of what the Lord did for me when I came up from Egypt" . . . So it shall be, when your son [*bincha*] asks you in time to come, saying, "What is this?" that you shall say to him, "By strength of hand the Lord brought us out of Egypt, out of the house of bondage. And it came to pass, when Pharaoh was stubborn about letting us go, that the Lord killed all the firstborn in the land of Egypt, both the firstborn of man and the firstborn of beast. Therefore I sacrifice to the Lord all the males that open the womb, but all the firstborn of my sons [*banay*] I redeem." (Exod 13:8, 14–15)

8. Poole, *Commentary*, 141.

9. Matthew Henry explained the parallel phrase in 13:14, "when thy son asketh thee," in these words:

> Children should be directed and encouraged to ask their parents questions concerning the things of God, a practice which would be perhaps of all others the most profitable way of catechising; and parents must furnish themselves with useful knowledge, that they may be ready always to give an answer to their enquiries. If ever the *knowledge of God cover the earth*, as the waters do the sea, the fountains of family-instruction must first be broken up.

Henry, *Commentary*, 113.

10. Brueggemann, *Creative Word*, 25–26. On how Deuteronomy 4 and other Old Testament texts recount the history of salvation to various audiences and generations, see House, "Examining the Narrative."

Note that both Exodus 12 and 13 impressed upon believing parents the necessity of catechizing their covenant children. But this was more than just catechizing them in a separate class or at home; it was catechizing by means of the public ritual of worship.[11] The purpose of parents catechizing their children was for a specific purpose, according to John Calvin: "that they may thus transmit the service of God to their descendants."[12] As Matthew Henry said, this catechizing is "a debt we owe . . . to the benefit of our children's souls, to tell them of the great works God has done for his church, both those which we have seen with our eyes done in our day and which we have heard with our ears and our fathers have told us."[13] Elsewhere, Matthew Henry commented: "Care must be taken in general to preserve the entail of religion among them, and to transmit the knowledge and worship of God to posterity."[14] Our forefathers understood these passages to apply to our children in our midst while we worship. We need to consider their arguments seriously.

Mount Sinai

After "the children of Israel had gone out of the land of Egypt," they traveled through "the wilderness of Sinai" until they "encamped there before the mountain" (Exod 19:1, 2). This was the occasion of the Lord taking Israel into a formal covenant relationship. There, all Israel—adults and children—gathered at the foot of Mount Sinai. Moses ascended the mountain and "went up to God" where the Lord called him to deliver his word to "the house of Jacob . . . the children of Israel" (Exod 19:3). The solemn and joyful

11. See also Deut 4:9–10, in which Moses spoke about the importance of worship and teaching a new generation of children. Those who were children at Horeb and had left the extravagance of Egypt now had to pass on the words and worship of the Lord to their children who would enter the promised land, inhabited by the Canaanites.

12. Calvin, *Commentaries on the Four Last Books of Moses*, 1:471; cf. Poole, *Commentary*, 144.

13. Henry, *Commentary*, 113.

14. Ibid., 241.

declaration was: "And you shall be to Me a kingdom of priests and a holy nation" (Exod 19:6). The solemn liturgy consisted of the Lord speaking and in response "all the people answered together and said, 'All that the Lord has spoken we will do'" (Exod 19:8).

When this liturgy ended, the Lord called the people to prepare themselves for another meeting in which this covenant would be symbolically ratified with the sprinkling of blood (Exod 24). As he charged Moses: "Go to the people and consecrate them today and tomorrow, and let them wash their clothes. And let them be ready for the third day. For on the third day the Lord will come down upon Mount Sinai in the sight of all the people" (Exod 19:10–11).

The narrative then transitions to recount the law that the Lord gave the people by the hands of Moses. This means that when Israel assembled to meet with the Lord and God gave them his law, their children would have heard Moses deliver the law. Of course, when the children heard the second commandment, "You shall not make for yourself a carved image" (Exod 20:4), they would have heard with special attention the words that applied to them: "For I, the Lord your God, am a jealous God, visiting the iniquity of the fathers *upon the children* [*baniym*] to the third and fourth generations of those who hate Me, but showing mercy to thousands, to those who love Me and keep My commandments" (Exod 20:5–6, emphasis added). The assembled children would have heard this law alongside their parents, but also with particular interest these words addressed to them in the fourth commandment, "Remember the Sabbath day, to keep it holy . . . In it you shall do no work: you, *nor your son* [*vu-bincha*], *nor your daughter* [*vu-bitecha*]" (Exod 20:8, 10), and especially in the fifth commandment, "Honor your father and your mother, that your days may be long in the land which the Lord your God is giving you" (Exod 20:12). This covenant at Sinai would later be renewed with all Israel as it crossed the Jordan River into the promised land in the days of Joshua (Josh 8:30–35).[15]

15. John Calvin concluded his comments on this passage with this striking line: "It added no little weight to the whole, that the children also were admitted as witnesses." Calvin, *Commentaries on the Book of Joshua*, 4:233.

National Festivals

Toward the end of Deuteronomy, Moses spoke of the worship service that occurred every seven years during the Feast of Tabernacles in which debts were forgiven. At this service, we notice, again, the presence of the church's children:

> So Moses wrote this law and delivered it to the priests, the sons of Levi, who bore the ark of the covenant of the Lord, and to all the elders of Israel. And Moses commanded them, saying: "At the end of every seven years, at the appointed time in the year of release, at the Feast of Tabernacles, when *all Israel* comes to appear before the Lord your God in the place which He chooses, you shall read this law before all Israel in their hearing. Gather the people together, men and women and little *ones* [*ve-hataph*], and the stranger who is within your gates, that they may hear and that they may learn to fear the Lord your God and carefully observe all the words of this law, and that *their children* [*vu-beneyhem*], who have not known it, may hear and learn to fear the Lord your God as long as you live in the land which you cross the Jordan to possess." (Deut 31:9–13, emphasis added)

At this service, the law of the Lord was to be read to all Israel, including men, women, children, and sojourners (Deut 31:11). The purpose of everyone assembling to hear the law was to fear the Lord and obey his law (Deut 31:12). Further, Moses said that those children "who have not known it"—for an unspecified reason—would also benefit by hearing and learning to fear the Lord. This was a national way of catechizing and evangelizing the covenant children of Israel. John Calvin picked up on this when he commented on the purpose of this ceremony being that children would "learn to fear the Lord your God" when he said:

> Finally, when their children are mentioned, reference is made to the propagation of sound doctrine, that the pure worship of God may continually be maintained. He therefore commands that the Law should be recited, not in one generation only, but as long as the status of the

people may last; and surely all God's servants ought to take care, that they may transmit to posterity what they have learnt themselves. Yet we must remark, that all doctrine which may have been handed down from their ancestors, is not here promiscuously commended; but God rather claims for Himself the entire authority, both towards the fathers and the children.[16]

We see children among the worshipping congregation at yet another national festival. In the days of Jehoshaphat, king of Judah, when the Moabites and Ammonites assembled for war against the southern kingdom of Judah, the king responded to this threat in the following way:

> And Jehoshaphat feared, and set himself to seek the Lord, and proclaimed a fast throughout all Judah. So Judah gathered together to ask help from the Lord; and from all the cities of Judah they came to seek the Lord. Then Jehoshaphat stood in the assembly of Judah and Jerusalem, in the house of the Lord, before the new court (2 Chron 20:3–5).

Jehoshaphat's decree was for a national, congregational fast "throughout all Judah," and all the people responded by coming "from all the cities of Judah . . . to seek the Lord." The narrative goes on to give more detail about those who assembled for the solemn fast:

> Now *all Judah, with their little ones* [*gam-tapham*]*, their wives, and their children* [*vu-beneyhem*], stood before the Lord . . . And he said, "Listen, *all you of Judah* and *you inhabitants of Jerusalem*, and you, King Jehoshaphat! Thus says the Lord to you: 'Do not be afraid nor dismayed because of this great multitude, for the battle is not yours, but God's. (2 Chron 20:13, 15, emphasis added)

"All Judah" was not merely the men, but included their wives and littlest children. They sought the Lord out in the open with their children, even as their enemies sought to attack them. This is

---

16. Calvin, *Commentaries on the Four Last Books of Moses*, 2:233.

why Matthew Poole described how this service must have moved the parents of these children, as "their eye, being upon their harmless and tender children, might affect their heart with a greater sense of their misery."[17] The Israelite parents became like their little children before the Lord—a theme we will see below in the teaching of Jesus.

Rebuilding the Temple

After King Hezekiah's days, the southern kingdom of Judah was taken into captivity into Babylon. After their exile, they were allowed to return to the promised land and begin the work of rebuilding their temple. When they returned, the entire assembly gathered for a worship service, especially to make confession of their sins: "Now while Ezra was praying, and while he was confessing, weeping, and bowing down before the house of God, a very large assembly of men, women, *and children* [*viy-ladiym*] gathered to him from Israel; for the people wept very bitterly" (Ezra 10:1; emphasis added). Here the inspired writer uses a different word for "children," *yeled*, yet it has the same meaning as the previous words used for little children. While Ezra confessed and wept for the people's sins that led them into captivity, not only did the men and women weep "bitterly," so did the little children.

The story of Scripture continues with the rebuilding of the temple foundation and altar. After this, the returned exiles gathered for another public service of worship. At that service, they heard the reading of the Law of God as in days of old. We read of the congregation that gathered for worship including children: "So Ezra the priest brought the Law before the assembly of men and women and all who could hear with understanding on the first day of the seventh month" (Neh 8:2). Regarding this text, Matthew Henry commented: "The persons that met were all the people, who were not compelled to come, but voluntarily gathered themselves together by common agreement, as one man: not only men came,

17. Poole, *Commentary*, 841.

but women and children, even as many as were capable of understanding what they heard." Henry continued with an important and powerful application for heads of households who brought their families with them to public worship: "Women and children have souls to save, and are therefore concerned to acquaint themselves with the word of God and attend on the means of knowledge and grace. Little ones, as they come to the exercise of reason, must be trained up in the exercises of religion."[18]

Later, at the dedication of the new wall of the temple, we read that Nehemiah gathered all the people for yet another worship service. The Levites were sought out so that the dedication would be with gladness, thanksgiving, and singing as accompanied by many instruments such as cymbals, psalteries, and harps (Neh 12:27). The narrative goes on to describe that service as the Levites "offered great sacrifices, and rejoiced, for God had made them rejoice with great joy; the women *and the children* [*ve-hayladiym*] also rejoiced, so that the joy of Jerusalem was heard afar off" (Neh 12:43). "God overlooks not," Henry said, "but graciously accepts, the honest zealous services of mean people, though there is in them little of art and they are far from being fine."[19]

New Testament

In turning from the Old to the New Testament, there are two classic examples of the place of children in the church that stand out for our consideration.

Jesus and Children

According to our Lord Jesus Christ, children belong to his kingdom. In Mark 10, we read the story of Jesus and his disciples leaving the town of Capernaum and coming to the region of Judea and the region beyond the Jordan (Mark 10:1). There, "as He was

18. Henry, *Commentary*, 634; cf. Poole, *Commentary*, 895.
19. Henry, *Commentary*, 640.

accustomed, He taught them" (Mark 10:1). After answering the Pharisees who sought to test and trap him by getting him to violate the law of God on the subject of divorce (Mark 10:2–9), he instructed his disciples on the same subject (Mark 10:10–12). It was then that people "brought little children (*paidia*) to Him; that He might touch them" (Mark 10:13).[20] The word used for "children" here may refer to children anywhere from infancy (Luke 1:59; 2:17) to children that are older and have the ability to talk (Luke 7:32). In response to these peoples' actions, Jesus' disciples "rebuked those who brought them" (Mark 10:13). Although this text does not occur in the context of a worship service, it does show Jesus' attitude toward having children in his presence and the presence of his people. In response to his own disciples' rebuke, Jesus "was greatly displeased and said to them, 'Let the little children [*paidia*] come to Me, and do not forbid them; for of such is the kingdom of God. Assuredly, I say to you, whoever does not receive the kingdom of God as a little child [*paidion*] will by no means enter it'" (Mark 10:14–15).

When Jesus said this, he was rebuking his disciples' adult arrogance in trying to shield him from what they saw as "insignificant" children. Instead, Jesus said, if we receive a child in Christ's name, we receive the Lord himself (Mark 9:36–37). Jesus is saying that these children belonged to him, and thus his adult disciples had to become like *them* to enter the kingdom of God—insignificant and useless in the eyes of the world, not claiming any inherent worth.

Because the kingdom of God belongs even to "such" as children, Jesus called upon his disciples to let them come to him.[21] Matthew Henry made the connection between children belonging to the covenant in the Old Testament and belonging to the kingdom in the New Testament when he applied this text in these words:

> He owned them as members of his church, as they had been of the Jewish church. He came to set up the *kingdom of God* among men, and took this occasion to declare that

20. See the parallel passage in Matthew 19:13–15.

21. John Calvin points out this fact as well in his comments on this text. *Harmony of the Gospels*, 2:251–52.

that kingdom admitted *little children* to be the subjects of it, and gave them a title to the privileges of subjects. Nay, the kingdom of God is to be kept up by such: they must be taken in when they are little children, that they may be secured for hereafter, to bear up the name of Christ.[22]

Jesus did not view children as a distraction to his disciples "getting something" out of his teaching of the Word. Neither should we view them as a hindrance to the preaching of the Word of God in our context of worship. In fact, Jesus went on to demonstrate the vital place of children in his midst as "He took them up in His arms, laid His hands on them, and blessed them" (Mark 10:16).

In Luke's Gospel we learn that as Jesus was making his way to Jerusalem, he was teaching, just as in Mark 10. Without introduction or transition, though, Luke simply mentioned that while Jesus was teaching, "they also brought infants (*ta brephē*) to Him that He might touch them" (Luke 18:15). Here Luke uses an even more specific word for infants as opposed to Mark's more general term for children. As in Mark's Gospel, we read, "When the disciples saw it, they rebuked them" (Luke 18:15). In response, Jesus manifested his attitude to children once again, calling out and saying, "Let the little children [*paidia*] come to Me, and do not forbid them; for of such is the kingdom of God. Assuredly, I say to you, whoever does not receive the kingdom of God as a little child [*paidion*] will by no means enter it" (Luke 18:16–17).

Another feature to note in Jesus' teaching is that in the traditional English text, the venerable translators of the King James Bible have Mark and Luke both saying "for of such" (*tōn gar toioutōn*), while all modern translations (NASB; ESV; NIV) use the phrase "to such." The KJV doesn't come across to us as strongly as the modern versions. The point that Jesus is teaching to his disciples is that because his kingdom belongs *to* these little children they are examples *of* his kingdom to the rest of the people God. This means that those who become childlike—with humble faith and with

22. Henry, *Commentary*, 1800. See also the comments by Lane, *Gospel of Mark*, 359–60.

filial reverence for their Father—will receive his kingdom. This is what Jesus taught his disciples in response to their question, "Who then is the greatest in the kingdom of heaven?" (Matt 18:1).

> Then Jesus called a little child [*paidion*] to Him, set him in the midst of them, and said, "Assuredly, I say to you, unless you are converted and become as little children [*paidia*], you will by no means enter the kingdom of heaven. Therefore whoever humbles himself as this little child [*paidion*] is the greatest in the kingdom of heaven. Whoever receives one little child [*paidion*] like this in My name receives Me." (Matt 18:2–5)

In practical terms, what we can say about Jesus' example of welcoming children into his midst and his words about them is, first, they are significant to Christ; second, they are not a hindrance or nuisance to Christ; and third, they can teach us a great deal about our relationship with Christ from watching them and worshipping together with them in the Lord's midst. As we see them sing, recite the creeds, pray, and join in the entirety of worship, we as adults and parents can learn *from* them because God's kingdom is full *of* them.[23] The idea behind Jesus' words in Matthew 18 and 19, Mark 10, and Luke 18 were already expressed in the words of Psalm 131 and sung by the people of God for a thousand years before our Lord came. They are also words that we must sing to apply Jesus' teaching to our hearts:

> Lord, my heart is not haughty,
> Nor my eyes lofty.
> Neither do I concern myself with great matters,
> Nor with things too profound for me.
> Surely I have calmed and quieted my soul,
> Like a weaned child with his mother;
> Like a weaned child *is* my soul within me.
> O Israel, hope in the Lord
> From this time forth and forever.

---

23. See the comments in Geldenhuys, *Gospel of Luke*, 454–56.

Paul and Children

The other New Testament example comes from the pen of the Apostle Paul. In two of his prison epistles, Ephesians 6:1–4 and Colossians 3:20, Paul gives pastoral instruction on the responsibility of children to their parents and their parents' responsibility to raise them as members of the Christian church. Notice how children are to obey their parents and how parents, especially fathers, are to raise their children:

> Children, obey your parents in the Lord, for this is right. "Honor your father and mother," which is the first commandment with promise: "that it may be well with you and you may live long on the earth." And you, fathers, do not provoke your children to wrath, but bring them up in the training and admonition of the Lord. (Eph 6:1–4)

> Children, obey your parents in all things, for this is well pleasing to the Lord. (Col 3:20)

In reading these words yet again, it is quite possible that you have overlooked the little phrase in Ephesians 6:1: "Children, obey your parents *in the Lord*." What is the significance of this for our discussion? All throughout Ephesians, the Apostle Paul uses this little preposition "in" with a variety of direct objects to describe the relationship between Christ and his people. For example, Paul speaks of those to whom he wrote as being "in" the following:

- "in Christ" (Eph 1:3, 10, 12, 20; 4:32)
- "in Christ Jesus" (Eph 1:1; 2:6, 7, 10, 13; 3:6)
- "in the Lord Jesus" (Eph 1:15)
- "in Jesus" (Eph 4:20)
- "in Christ Jesus our Lord" (Eph 3:11)
- "in the Lord" (Eph 2:21; 4:17; 5:8; 6:10, 21)
- "in Him/Himself" (Eph 1:4, 7, 9, 10, 11, 13; 2:15)

The Nursery of the Holy Spirit

- "in the Beloved" (Eph 1:6)

- "in whom" (Eph 1:13; 2:21, 22; 3:12, 13)

Let me clearly state what this does not mean first. When Paul addressed the churches in Ephesus and Colossae as "the saints who are in Ephesus" (Eph 1:1) and "the saints and faithful brethren in Christ who are in Colossae" (Col 1:2), and when he addressed them all, including children, as being "in the Lord," he was not saying that everyone in those churches were necessarily saved. What he was saying was that all whom he addressed were "in" the Lord's body, his church—both parents and their children.

So what do these verses have to do with bringing our children into worship? Again, my argument is an implicit one, by way of example. Paul's letters would have been read in the public services of the church. As he says in Colossians 4:16: "Now when this epistle is read among you, see that it is read also in the church of the Laodiceans, and that you likewise read the epistle from Laodicea." This example, then, means that when the Epistle to the Colossians was read, the children whom Paul addressed in Colossians 3:20 reasonably seem to have been present among the assembly to hear those words. In being present for the hearing of God's Word, new covenant children are just like children in Israel, who had been at the foot of Mount Sinai.[24] To put it in a provocative form: imagine if the practice of so many churches today, which have children's church during the entirety of corporate worship or which dismiss children to children's church just before the reading and preaching of the Word, were going on in Paul's day. While Paul's letters were being read to the congregations, his practical exhortations to the church's children to obey their parents would have fallen upon deaf ears if all those children were not present. Again, I know this is an argument from silence as the text does not say all of this, but it is a reasonable reading of the text.

When Paul says, "Children, obey your parents in the Lord," he is saying no small thing, then. As the children in the Old Testament were related to the people of God via their parents, so too are

24. Lincoln, *Ephesians*, 403.

32

children in the New Testament. This is why Paul goes on to quote the fifth commandment, "Honor your father and mother," and says that it still applies to children in the new covenant.

Paul also addresses the place of our children in the church in a passage already mentioned: 1 Corinthians 7:14. Here he speaks of the broken family in which only one spouse is a believer. What does this mean for their home and their children? "For the unbelieving husband is sanctified by the wife, and the unbelieving wife is sanctified by the husband; otherwise your children would be unclean, but now they are holy." Again, this means that the family unit is "sanctified" even if only the husband or the wife is a believer. Hence, his conclusion is that the children are "sanctified" as a result of a single believing parent. These divided families are still Christian families and their children are Christians, "sanctified" to the Lord just as the sons and daughters of Israel were a "holy seed" (Ezra 9:2; Isa 6:13). God chooses to work through families, even broken ones. What a great word of hope to those of us affected by the Fall with the tragedy of a broken family! Yet out of our brokenness the Lord makes his treasure! If this describes you, let the Lord's word to the Apostle Paul about his strength in weakness remind you of what God can do in your family:

> And He said to me, "My grace is sufficient for you, for My strength is made perfect in weakness." Therefore most gladly I will rather boast in my infirmities, that the power of Christ may rest upon me. Therefore I take pleasure in infirmities, in reproaches, in needs, in persecutions, in distresses, for Christ's sake. For when I am weak, then I am strong (2 Cor 12:9–10).

In conclusion, what do Jesus' and Paul's words mean for the place of our children in the public worship of the church? In summary, because believers belong to the church their children receive the many blessings of this relationship such as worshiping with their parents, hearing the preaching of the Word, participating in family worship at home, joining in the prayers of the church, experiencing the fellowship of the people of God, and being under the spiritual discipleship of the pastors and elders of the church.

The Nursery of the Holy Spirit

Since our children belong to the church and since they have been included in its worship over the millennia, therefore they ought to belong in our worship.

3

Parenting in the Pew

AFTER ALL THAT I'VE said, I want to get to some practical application. How do *you* begin the practice of worshipping together with your children? And if you already do so, how can you refresh your practice of this? One Reformed forefather cut to the chase and exhorted his congregation in the following way:

> Take your children to church at an early age, even though they do not yet understand anything. Accustom them to service of God and to the holy worship services—to sit still and to be along with you, just as in olden times the Israelites took their children along with them to the solemn rites of religion. Do not permit them to sleep, to play, or to speak to you in church. Do not give them anything to eat in church, but when they comes out of the church with you, then give them something if they sat still.[1]

This might sound harsh and rigid to us, but the practical point was the same: you begin this practice or refresh your commitment to this practice by just doing it. More recently, Robbie Castleman published a warm and joyful approach to this, entitled, *Parenting in the Pew*. In this chapter I want to continue the work

1. Koelman, *Duties of Parents*, 49. See also Hildersham, *Dealing with Sin*, 18–19.

of our forefathers and this fine recent book by offering some helpful and practical application to help those of you who have never included children in worship with you and to refresh those of you who are looking for new ways to keep going in this practice.[2]

The Necessity of Training Our Children to Worship

Parents, if I may be direct and to the point: I hope you realize that the most important thing you can ever train your child to do is to worship the Triune God of grace. The first and most important thing I can say to you is that you must embrace your responsibility. You are called by God to train your children to serve the Lord.[3] I am not writing about giving your children a "secular" training, that is, an education in the things of this world such as reading, writing, and arithmetic, but a responsibility to give your children a spiritual training. Remember what Paul said: "Fathers . . . bring them up in the training and admonition *of the Lord*" (Eph 6:4). Matthew Henry's comments on this text are apropos as he did not miss this point:

> It is the great duty of parents to be careful in the education of their children: Not only bring them up, as the brutes do, taking care to provide for them; but bring them up in nurture and admonition, in such a manner as is suitable to their reasonable natures. Nay, *not only bring them up as men*, in nurture and admonition, *but as Christians*, in the admonition of the Lord. Let them have a religious education. Instruct them to fear sinning; and inform them of, and excite them to, the whole of their duty towards God.[4]

This has been the responsibility of parents throughout the ages (e.g., Deut 6:1–9). In fact, Robbie Castleman speaks of the foregoing examples we have examined from the life of Israel,

---

2. See also Walker, "Attendance of Children in Public Worship."

3. Castleman, *Parenting in the Pew*, 17.

4. Henry, *Commentary*, 2318, emphasis added.

saying, "God had to train the nation of Israel to worship."[5] The Lord gave Israel numerous details about worship in the Law (e.g., Exod 10:26; Lev 1–7), as God was their father, training his young child until it reached maturity in the new covenant. As the Apostle Paul says, "the law was our tutor" (Gal 3:24), that is, an instructor, a teacher. We, too, can look to the Lord and his Word for guidance.

The necessity of training our children to worship the Lord is urgent. The Barna Research Group's recent study entitled "Teenagers Embrace Religion but Are Not Excited about Christianity" illustrates this urgency.[6] While this study showed that more teens than adults are broadly involved in church-based activities, with more than seven out of ten teens engaged in some church-related effort in a typical week, the study revealed a fearful future:

> When asked to estimate the likelihood that they will continue to participate in church life once they are living on their own, levels dip precipitously, to only about one out of every three teens. Placed in context, that stands as the lowest level of expected participation among teens recorded by Barna Research in more than a decade. If the projections pan out, this would signal a substantial decline in church attendance occurring before the close of this new decade.

We must not and cannot wait. We must seize the opportunity to train our children to worship and to raise them in the nurture and admonition of the Lord *now*. I am arguing for including children in public worship as a central component of that training.

Difficult, but Desirable

As a pastor who planted a Reformed church in a southern California beach community with no other Reformed churches in the area, and as a father myself, I know the difficulty of squirmy

---

5. Castleman, *Parenting in the Pew*, 19.
6. Barna, "Teenagers Embrace Religion."

and noisy children in worship.[7] I experience it on a weekly basis. Whether it is with those who worship with us for the first time as visitors or with members who have children and begin to bring them into worship, this is a difficult and anxious experience. As a congregation, we are fully aware that having children in the worship service can look strange to those accustomed to having their children go off to their own age-appropriate church or class. As a mother, pastor's wife, and college professor, Castleman expresses this well in her excellent and helpful book:

> Worship can be one of the times when we parents would like to pay attention to something other than our children. Kids can be distracting, aggravating and embarrassing in church. Parenthood can make sitting in a pew a lot of work. Paying attention to our children can make us less attentive to the service. The temptations to just stay home, or at least keep the kids out of the sanctuary, are real. It's hard to pay attention to God and children at the same time.[8]

This is why as churches, we need to accept each other in this difficult task of training our children to worship. The older members need to encourage the younger members. And if a child needs to be taken out for discipline, we should not be offended, but encouraged by the effort to raise children as worshippers.

While worshipping with our children is difficult and often very exhausting work, it is desirable. Keep in perspective the eternal blessings that make your perseverance worthwhile. When you remember the purpose of "the Lord's Day" (Rev 1:10), the earthly and temporal difficulties of children in worship are put into their heavenly and eternal perspective. The Lord's Day is not only a day of earthly, temporary, and physical rest (which may even seem impossible when you have little children), but it is also a day in which our time in worship is time in the presence of the Triune God of grace. Therefore it is a day of heavenly, eternal, and spiritual rest.[9]

7. See Riddlebarger, "Squirming and Noisy Children."

8. Castleman, *Parenting in the Pew*, 15–16.

9. For a brief explanation of the Lord's Day, see Hyde, "Primer on the Lord's

When you remember the nature of public worship is not merely what *we do* and what *we get out of* it, but instead first and foremost God's service to us, then all the difficulties are put into their heavenly and eternal perspective.[10] God's grace is the priority in worship as he serves us by bringing us into communion with our Lord Jesus Christ in the power of the Holy Spirit. He does this by using the external means of the preaching of the Word of God, the celebration of baptism and the Lord's Supper, and prayer. The Lord's service to us brings us spiritual rest and refreshment. His service to us, then, creates in us and elicits from us our response as we serve him by praising him in song, prayer, offering, and even by serving each other in fellowship.

Let me put it before you in a very pointed question: do you believe your children interfere with *God's* purpose on *his* day to serve us? We may naturally be inclined to think this way. Jesus knows that. That's why he brought little ones into the assembly of his disciples. As we saw above, because Jesus' disciples, too, thought that children interfered with the Lord's purposes, rebuking those who brought little children to Jesus (Mark 10:13). Thankfully, our Lord Jesus did not think as his disciples did:

> But when Jesus saw it, He was greatly displeased and said to them, "Let the little children come to Me, and do not forbid them; for of such is the kingdom of God. Assuredly, I say to you, whoever does not receive the kingdom of God as a little child will by no means enter it." And He took them up in His arms, laid His hands on them, and blessed them. (Mark 10:14–16; Matt 19:13–15; Luke 18:15–17; cf. Pss 8:2; 78:1–8)

We should welcome children into our services with us because, like the children above, we desire our little ones to come into Jesus' presence to receive his spiritual nourishment even as we need it.

Day." For longer treatments, see Campbell, *On the First Day*; Dennison, *Market Day of the Soul*.

10. Hyde, *What to Expect*, 5–10.

Reorienting Our Minds

I do not want you to think that your responsibility is to desire that your children "go to church" or simply sit quietly so as not to be a distraction. We must reorient our minds, then, about what we are trying to accomplish in training our children. What is the difference in "going to church" versus "going to worship" or "going to the Lord's service?" To go to church conveys the idea of being passive, of going out of obligation, and of being overly somber. To go to worship or the Lord's service is to be a participant, to go out of the "liberty" Christ has won for us (Gal 5:1), and to go with joy: "I was glad when they said to me, 'Let us go into the house of the Lord'" (Ps 122:1). As Castleman says, "Parenting in the pew can be a hassle. Or it can be holy. It depends on who we are and how we see ourselves. Do we sit with our children 'in church' or 'in worship?'"[11] We go to worship because it is the supreme pinnacle of our life as Christians. We go to "serve the Lord with fear, and [to] rejoice with trembling" (Ps 2:11); we go with gratitude to "serve God acceptably with reverence and godly fear. For our God is a consuming fire" (Heb 12:28–29); we go with eagerness and expectation as the Lord of heaven and earth meets with us to serve us in grace and to call us to serve him in gratitude. The prophet Zechariah described worship in the new covenant like this: "In those days ten men from every language of the nations shall grasp the sleeve of a Jewish man, saying, 'Let us go with you, for we have heard that God is with you" (Zech 8:23). Since God is with his people especially in holy worship, let us focus our minds upon him and bring our children to that great meeting.

The Biggest Stumbling Block

Another practical point you need to consider seriously is that the greatest stumbling block for your children in worship is not that they are bored or because nothing is "at their level," but that you as their parents do not convey in words and deeds that you cherish

---

11. Castleman, *Parenting in the Pew*, 30.

holy worship. Keep this saying in mind: worship is better caught than taught. What does this mean? It means that our children learn by participating in worship more than by our explanations about worship. Therefore your children can feel the difference between duty and delight. They will pick up from you a dour attitude if you have a dour attitude. They will come to believe that worship is not that important if you do not show them that it is important. As a parent, you are the greatest example to your children of the meaning and value of worshipping the Lord. Having your children with you in worship allows them to be taught about worship by what they have caught in worship as their eager eyes watch you model this Lord's Day after Lord's Day. As you follow the example of the early church by "continu[ing] steadfastly in the apostles' doctrine and fellowship, in the breaking of bread, and in prayers" (Acts 2:42), your children should see how you listen hungrily to the Word of God read and preached, how you "greet the friends by name" (3 John 15) as well as "entertain strangers" (Heb 13:2), that is, show hospitality to those who visit the church, how you reverently partake of the bread and cup of the Lord's Supper, and how you bow your head earnestly in prayer and sing out your praise to God with sheer joy in your face. You must love to worship your God so that your children will learn to love him through the liturgy [order of service] your church utilizes. After all, you cannot preach what you do not possess or have not first preached to yourself.

Understanding Our Children

What I said in the opening of this book about developmental psychology changing the church's attitude about her children from a liturgical point of view to an educational point of view should not be seen as throwing the baby out with the bathwater. We do need to know how our children learn and develop so that we may learn to train them to worship better.[12]

12. This section is indebted to Sandell, *Including Children in Worship*, 25–28.

For example, parents may wonder at the wisdom of including children under the age of two in worship. No doubt some of
these children may be restless and distracting to those around
them, but as they grow into toddlers, they come to worship with
the following:

- a rather limited attention span
- seemingly unlimited energy
- a growing curiosity about *everything*

While these ingredients can combine to test the patience of
parents, there are several things parents can do to make the child's
experience and their own more relaxed and worshipful. The pre-
school and kindergarten-aged child (3–5) brings some great new
abilities to worship with them, such as:

- a greater capacity for attentive listening to the sermon
- an increasing ability to sing the songs, listen to the Bible, and
  follow the order of service in the bulletin
- the ability to organize and memorize information and to
  write that information down

Obviously, as our children grow, they grow in their ability
to worship. We as their parents need to be sensitive and aware of
the particular capacities and abilities of our children. With these
abilities in mind, we as Christian parents can train our beloved
children toward a greater participation in the church's worship.
Having sensitivity to your own particular children's abilities and
needs can help you make public worship a more pleasant and
meaningful experience for you, them, and the entire congregation.[13] And when the entire congregation understands that every
parent and every child is at a different place with all of this, we will
be equipped to be more patient and graceful to the difficulties.

13. On this, see Ng and Thomas, *Children in the Worshipping Community*,
and Sandell, *Including Children in Worship*.

ABC's for Parents of Children

Let me now offer a basic outline for you as parents (or expectant parents) as you train yourself to train your children for the wonder of worship in the presence of God. Keep in mind that this is my list, meaning it is by no means exhaustive. Your family and congregational circumstances may necessitate adding to, subtracting from, or modifying the things that I list below for your own use.

Training at Home

The earliest training ground for worship is the home. For example, you can train your toddler to pray in public worship by sitting quietly and holding hands for just a moment while you ask God's blessing on a meal. Train your toddler to listen to a sermon by sitting on your lap while you read a Bible story and by answering the questions you ask of them about the story. Train them to sing some of the familiar songs from church by singing them at home. In our home, we do this before we put our children to bed. After a while, they not only learn some songs, but they also begin to sing along and even request their favorites. All of this and other aspects that occur in family prayer can train a child for what they need to learn to do on the Lord's Day.[14]

Using Nursery

Whether your congregation provides a nursery, childcare, or a cry-room, here are some thoughts to consider. First, as much as possible, try to keep your nursery-aged child in worship, as this teaches them to be in worship from the earliest age. Second, use whatever

14. Although this book is focused on the place of our children in worship, one should also consult available articles and books on the Reformed practice of family catechism and prayer: Alexander, *Thoughts on Family Worship*; Beeke, *Bringing the Gospel to Covenant Children*, *Family Worship*, and *Family at Church*; Hyde, "Little Parish"; Johnson, *Family Worship Book*; Van Dyken, *Rediscovering Catechism*; Whitney, *Family Worship*.

service is available only when you have to. You do not want to make it a crutch when the service runs long on a given Lord's Day or when your child gets restless so as to communicate that you stay in worship only as long as it seems interesting or until your child wants to go play. Third, there will be times when your child gets restless or noisy, despite your best efforts. If your child just will not be quiet, take him/her out for the sake of quick discipline and for the sake of the other worshipers. In my congregation, the back area of the sanctuary is reserved for parents with young children who are loud or having a difficult Sunday. Even if you stay in such an area, treat your child as if you were still in the sanctuary among the rest of the congregation—praying, singing, reciting, and listening to the Word. And if you need to utilize whatever childcare is provided, feel free to do so without any shame. Remember, whether your church has a nursery, childcare, or a cry room, it is there to help you temporarily as you train your little ones.[15]

Preparing for Worship

It is also important as parents to get your family into the habit of preparing for worship. Since the Lord's Day is the "Christian Sabbath" (WCF 21.7; WLC, Q&A 116; WSC, Q&A 59), "we are to prepare our hearts, and with such foresight, diligence, and moderation, to dispose and seasonably dispatch our worldly business, that we may be the more free and fit for the duties of that day" (WLC, Q&A 117). Our hearts and our bodies must be prepared to "come before His presence with thanksgiving" (Ps 95:2; cf. 100:2). Here are several ways to prepare ahead of time for the Lord's Day:

- Get enough rest so that you are able to engage in the worship of God.

- Have a "song of the week" or "song of the month" as a family, or even better, as a congregation. This encourages the whole family and congregation to learn the same songs.

---

15. On this, see Brown, "Cry for the Cry Room."

- Read the Scripture text(s) that will be read on Sunday before you come to the service with your children. If your church's liturgy is not posted on the church website or sent out via e-mail, just ask the pastor. Since repetition is the mother of skills, a little one's face really lights up when he/she hears familiar words from the pulpit.

- You may also work on preparing your little child to participate by choosing one part of the worship service at a time and building on that over the weeks and months to follow.

You can also prepare for the worship service on the Lord's Day itself. Here are a few examples:

- Arrive with plenty of time to spare.

- If you have little children, consider sitting near the front of the sanctuary so that your child can clearly see the liturgical furniture—pulpit, font, and table.

- Talk about what may be a special part of the service this week: a baptism, an ordination, the Lord's Supper. You can even prepare in the pew by taking the regular elements of the service and making them part of the anticipation. "We've been reading about Joseph at home this week. What do you think the pastor will say about him?" "What might we be singing this morning?" "Maybe we can sit next to a visitor or elderly member and help them with their songbook so they can worship better, too."

Goals and Requirements

A part of preparation is setting goals and requirements for your family and your children as it relates to their presence in the service. As my wife's college volleyball team motto said: "Fail to plan, plan to fail." Having a game plan will set the stage for success in training your children to worship. And do not forget that these goals need to be communicated to your children, especially the older children.

- Sit or stand when the service calls for it.

- Sit up straight and still—not lounging or fidgeting or crawling around—and be respectful toward God and the worshipers around you.

- Keep Bible, hymnal, and bulletin papers as quiet as possible.

- Stay awake. Sleeping communicates that worship is not important. Taking notes or drawing helps for little ones.

- Look toward the front, not around or behind.

- No bathroom breaks during the service. Leaving communicates that worship is casual.

Participating in the Liturgy

Having prepared for the Lord's Day you are ready for worship. Now you need to help your children participate in the liturgy that your church uses. As age allows, give them a bulletin / prayer book, songbook, and a Bible as it helps a child feel like a participant in the service. Make it a habit to join your child in reading or reciting short prayers, responses, and Scripture recitations in worship, such as the Lord's Prayer, Apostles' Creed, Ten Commandments, and other parts of the liturgy in your particular service. Feel free to whisper quietly to your children during the service about what is going on. Explain things to them and ask them questions. This helps them engage.

Participating in Prayer

One way you can teach your children to participate in the prayers offered in worship, especially any pastoral/intercessory prayers, is by paying attention to and participating in those prayers. As Koelman said to his congregation:

Charge your children to listen carefully to the prayers of the ministers before and after the sermons and catechism lessons, for in these prayers they will regularly hear all sorts of things, expressions, and "grounds" (at least if the ministers do not use formulary prayers, either from a book or composed by themselves). Ask them what they have observed in those prayers, how the ministers confess sins, how they pray for grace and forgiveness, how they implore God on behalf of the county and the church, ministers and authorities, the sick and the wretched, and tell them that they too must pray in that way as their understanding permits.[16]

The point is that you need to teach your children from an early age that the pastor's prayers are not a time for them to fall asleep, but a time for them to learn respect for the Lord. This may begin with sitting quietly for a moment when they are very little, to holding hands and closing eyes for a minute or two as they get older, and eventually to engaging in the entire prayer.

Participating in the Word

In order to participate in the reading and preaching of the Word, your children first need an open Bible before them. If you do not have a Bible for them yet, use a pew Bible. During the reading of the Word, have your children listen and maybe even circle the words in their Bible that stand out, that they heard in the songs, or that they remember from preparing to worship.

The beginning of the sermon is the signal for your older children to begin note taking. Taking notes grows up as the child does. At first, your younger child may scribble or doodle. They may draw a picture of what they hear in the sermon. Individual words or names trigger individual pictures. You might pick out a word that will be used frequently in the sermon; have the child listen carefully and make a check mark in his "notes" each time he hears the word. For older children, taking notes is done upon a special

16. Koelman, *Duties of Parents*, 97–98.

pad used just for weekly worship. Before you might expect it, he will probably be outlining the sermon and noting whole concepts. As Koelman said of children between six and twelve years of age:

> When they attend church, they should not only remember a few things to take home with them but, while they are in church, also take notes, as much as possible, of the sermons. Teach them how to distinguish the different parts of the sermon: the introduction, the division of the material, the explanation of the text, the teaching that flows from it, the prooftexts, the course of the argument, and the application. Show them how the application is designed to rebuke, to warn, to examine oneself (at this point the marks of genuineness are usually treated), to comfort, to admonish and exhort, in which connection the grounds for mercy and means of grace come up.[17]

Participating in the Offering

One of the first ways you can involve your child in worship is by allowing them to participate by giving the family's weekly tithe and offering. As they get older, you will also need to teach them the meaning of giving as well as to give of their own money. One of the things my wife and I have stressed with our children is that when they give the offering, they are to say, "Thank you, God." Teaching them what the offering is with a short recitation that they can say from an early age reinforces week after week our gratitude to God.

Participating in Baptism

Finally, another element of worship that you can teach your child to participate in is baptism. First, prepare your child beforehand and explain that there is going to be a baptism. This leads to great questions about what baptism is all about. Second, sit up close to the front of the church on these Sundays, let them stand in the aisle

---

17. Koelman, *Duties of Parents*, 57.

so that they can see, or even hold up little ones so that they can witness the administration of the sacrament. Third, after the service, walk them up and show them the font/baptismal, which will elicit from them some of the most amazing questions you will ever be asked. As my oldest son once asked me as I showed him the font, from which the glass bowl for water had been removed, revealing the hollow space, "Daddy, does the baby go inside there?"

Applying Worship

Worship does not end when the service ends and you return home. You have to work at applying worship to your children. Do this by talking to your children about the service in the car on the way home, over lunch, and throughout the day while it is fresh in their memories. Discuss what they saw, what they heard, and what they did. Also, take time to answer questions about worship that they may have. Especially talk to your children about the Word of God that was preached as well as what went on in the entire service on the way home. If your church celebrates any of the days of the church calendar, discuss the meaning and point of these days—Jesus Christ.[18]

One of the greatest and simplest of things you can do to parent your children in the pew is to enthusiastically express your gladness at having your children in worship with you. And if you have children sitting around your pew, be sure to do the same with them as well to spread the joy of parenting in the pew.

Liturgy as Catechism

Let me bring the practical advice above together into one main thought. I want to conclude this chapter by speaking to you about the liturgy, or order of worship, your church uses being itself a catechism instructor, or teacher, for your children. Most of us

18. For an example, see the colorfully illustrated book by Boling, *Come Worship with Me.*

understand that to become skillful in any aspect of life, we must repeat something over and over again. As men, we are not born good husbands and good fathers; instead, it takes practice and learning—sometimes the hard way—over time. For example, a good husband repeatedly hugs and kisses his wife before they part in the morning, when they reunite in the early evening, and before they go to bed at night. Marriage experts do not see this as boring repetition, but rather as a healthy practice. In a word, repetition is the mother of skills. This is why repetition is not necessarily dead, while spontaneity is not necessarily good, although some of us may have been taught otherwise.

"Liturgy," or the order, acts, words, and ceremonies in public worship, are a key instructor of us and our children. Now before you react in saying, "Did you say 'liturgy'?" let me assure you that this is no four-letter word, although, like me, you may have been taught that. Instead, our English word "liturgy" comes from an ancient Greek word, *leitourgia*, which can generally mean any kind of service, but specifically speaks of religious service. Every church, therefore, uses a liturgy. It is not something only Roman Catholicism or dead, "traditional" churches use, but something used in every worship service in the world. Whether or not a particular church has a structured or loose service, or whether a "liturgy" is printed in the bulletin and followed, every church has a liturgy every time they worship. Like a teacher that asks a question and like a student that responds with an answer—what is called the Socratic method[19]—the liturgy of every church catechizes its worshippers.[20]

19. For an excellent exposition of catechesis, see Sayers, "Lost Tools of Learning." See also Clark, "Why We Memorize the Catechism."

20. The word "catechism" comes from a biblical verb *katēcheō* which occurs eight times in the New Testament. Luke uses this word twice for being instructed generally (Acts 21:21, 24) and twice for being instructed specifically in the Christian faith: Apollos was "instructed [*katēchēmenos*] in the way of the Lord" (Acts 18:25) and Luke wrote to Theophilus, "That you may have certainty concerning the things you have been taught" (Luke 1:4; *katēchēthēs*). Paul uses this verb four times exclusively for religious instruction. He spoke of the Jews "being instructed [*katēchoumenos*] from the law" (Rom 2:18). He spoke of the instruction Christian's receive: "Nevertheless, in church I would rather speak five words with my mind in order to instruct [*katēchēsō*] others,

As I said earlier, life skills are learned by repetition. This is also the case with religious skills such as learning to worship with the people of God. Repetitiveness is a virtue, not a vice. For instance, in a recent educational book, the field of cognitive psychology has been harvested and applied to mathematics instruction. Research studies show that it takes in excess of twenty-four separate sessions of repeated practice to have an 80 percent competence in a mathematical skill.[21] The authors of this book conclude their survey of this research in saying that "learning new content, then, does not happen quickly. It requires practice spread out over time."[22]

Worship requires practice over time, as well. The liturgy should be heard from cradle to grave, from birthing bed to death-bed. In times of great joy, what better words to sing than those of the Reformed Doxology, "Praise God from whom all blessings flow"? In times of great sorrow, is there anything so comforting as praying, "Our Father, who art in heaven"? In times of doubt, the words "I believe in God, the Father Almighty" are fitting to help bolster failing faith. In times of repentance, the liturgy has taught us to cry out, "Lord have mercy on us, Christ have mercy on us, Lord have mercy on us."

By including the corporate participation of the entire church including children, liturgy teaches us that all, young and old, belong to the church. Liturgical worship is active, participatory worship. Children can hear it and learn it even before they read, and see it later with their own eyes upon the pages of the hymnal or bulletin as they begin to be able to read. For example, a four-year-old child can recite the Apostles' Creed with the local church and the church universal even before being able to read it in the hymnal or bulletin. Christianity is not a religion of adults for adults. Christianity is a churchly religion.

---

than ten thousand words in a tongue" (1 Cor 14:19). He spoke to the Galatians, saying, "One who is taught [*katēchoumenos*] the word must share all good things with the one who teaches" (Gal 6:6; *katēchounti*).

21. Marzano et al., *Classroom Instruction*, 66. The primary research may be found in Newell and Rosenbloom, "Mechanisms of Skill Acquisition," and Anderson, *Learning and Memory*.

22. Marzano, *Classroom Instruction*, 68.

So what does this all mean for your congregation, especially if you do not follow a historic Reformed liturgy? First, we need not be ashamed of using set forms of worship and set liturgical responses.[23] Set forms are not evil or binding on our conscience *if the forms are biblical.* Set forms actually communicate to the unbeliever what we believe and what they need to believe as well. Set forms do not quench the Spirit or cause "dead orthodoxy," but in fact have been used by the Spirit in the church for ages and communicate to us what the Spirit is saying to the church. Using a set form of worship with set words from the minister and responses from the congregation can benefit a congregation. Boredom and a lack of enthusiasm are not the fault of a good liturgy, which is saturated with the Word of God, but it is our fault—our lack of preparation for worship, our lack of appreciation, our lack of reverence. In fact, changing your church's order of worship just for the sake of change can actually do more harm than good. For example, in my first year or so of planting the church I now pastor, I would change the order of worship and the words in the liturgy almost every week. Finally, a father of two young daughters came to me and said that his children were confused and lost in worship as well as not able to participate as much because they didn't know what would be said that particular Sunday. Utilizing set forms of worship actually equips the people of God, especially children, to participate in worship with understanding and passion. By memorizing what to say, there is an expectation to say those words when they are said in the liturgy.

Second, we need to help those under our care understand why we are using the liturgy we use by teaching them the meaning of it. As pastors and teachers, we need to highlight various aspects of the liturgy in our sermons and Christian education programs. Tying our theology into our liturgy is natural and necessary. What greater time to speak of why we read the law, confess our sins, and receive forgiveness every week in our worship than when we

---

23. This is in contrast to Johnson, *Leading in Worship,* 17, who says that fixed forms of prayer and responses in worship crowd out free prayer, are artificial, difficult, and not Reformed.

preach and teach on a text like Psalm 51? When we are teaching a catechism class on Peter's confession of Christ in Matthew 16, what better time to speak to them about why we recite the Apostles' and/ or Nicene Creeds in worship? Doing this in our instruction also helps children and adults put the things together that they read in the Bible and their church's catechism like pieces of a puzzle.

Conclusion

Learning that repetition is the mother of skills may take some time to get used to, but it will be rewarded with a worshipping congregation filled with young and old. Just think about what your congregation will know and be able to say back to God in any circumstance of life after learning your church's theology methodically and surely over the years by repetition. Think also about the children in your congregation now, who will one day be the leaders of your church and the parents of another generation of children. They are not too young to begin learning the weekly pattern of worship that correctly reflects our theology, but must begin now to join with us.

CONCLUSION

A Plea for Children in Worship

By now I pray you are beginning to see how Christians have historically kept their children in the service of worship and how that practice is rooted in the Scriptures of both the Old and New Testaments. Let me conclude with a plea for *you* to include the children of your church in public worship. The addition of children to a family and to a congregation is a tremendous blessing as well as responsibility. I say this to you who will have children, as you prepare for life with them in the future. I say this to you with children, who may not currently join you in the service. I say this to entire congregations that are thinking of how best to worship the Lord and train children in that wonderful experience before the throne of grace. Not only is this consistent with the examples of the Old and New Testaments, but let me plead with you to include your children for four beneficial reasons.

First, your children belong to the body of Christ in one way or another, and public worship is a chief manifestation of that fact. Let them in; show them they belong from the earliest age. I cannot tell you what an amazing thing it is to look out over a congregation and see grandparents, parents, and children of all ages worshipping their Lord together, sitting together, and engaging in the sermon together. It is a sad fact that we live in an age in which so many of the church's children are leaving and never returning when they go to college after years and years of being kept out of worship. I have seen and heard the experience of many pastors and parents who grieved that one of the reasons their children left the church was because they never felt they belonged, they never had a sense of faithful ownership of what happened in church. Bringing them into the full life of the local church is a means of giving them ownership of the faith and a place to belong with fellow sinners.

Second, public worship as the nursery of the Holy Spirit is the context in which he creates true, saving faith. Bringing your children into worship is to bring them into the powerful presence of the Holy Spirit. It is the Spirit who creates faith and converts hearts chiefly through the preaching ministry of the gospel: "So then faith comes by hearing, and hearing by the word of God" (Rom 10:17). This is the heart of the matter. Our children have the same spiritual needs as everyone else in the world: they need their sins to be washed by the blood and Spirit of Christ. Your children need to be born again; they need the gift of faith to embrace Jesus as their Savior. If this is the case, bring them in where the Holy Spirit does that work—public worship where the gospel is preached (Rom 10:14–17).

The hearing of the Word is a blessing because the Word of God is his living voice to his people. Public worship is the ordinary means whereby God meets with his people and brings them his saving grace. "What are the outward means whereby Christ communicates to us the benefits of his mediation? The outward and ordinary means whereby Christ communicates to his church the benefits of his mediation, are all his ordinances; especially the word, sacraments, and prayer; all which are made effectual to the elect for their salvation" (WLC, Q&A 154). If we want our covenant children to embrace "the promise . . . to you and to your children" (Acts 2:39) they need to be with us, at our side, while God serves us in grace in the church's public services.

As we bring our children to participate in worship with us, they not only hear the Word, but they are also placed in the context where the Spirit of God works. The Westminster Larger Catechism says this about the Word preached and the benefits it conveys:

> How is the word made effectual to salvation?
>
> The spirit of God maketh the reading, but especially the preaching of the word, an effectual means of enlightening, convincing, and humbling sinners; of driving them out of themselves, and drawing them unto Christ; of conforming them to his image, and subduing them to his will; of strengthening them against temptations and corruptions; of building them up in grace, and establishing their hearts in holiness and comfort through faith unto salvation (WLC, Q&A 155).

The Spirit uses the preaching of the Word to convert sinners ("enlightening, convincing, and humbling sinners"), to create faith in sinners so that they will embrace Jesus ("of driving them out of themselves, and drawing them unto Christ"), and to conform sinners to their Lord's precious image in holiness ("of conforming them to his image, and subduing them to his will; of strengthening them against temptations and corruptions; building them up in grace, and establishing their hearts in holiness and comfort through faith unto salvation").[1] They need this ministry and public worship is the greatest place this is available.

In saying this, I do want to acknowledge that the reason many parents desire "age-appropriate" instruction for their children of the church's public services is rooted in their deep love and concern for the spiritual well-being of their children. This is a love and concern that all Christian parents should have and it is commendable. And because of it, we as parents should want our children in the best place for their spiritual lives to grow. That place is where preaching is heard, because God promises that it is the ordinary means of the Holy Spirit to bring sinners to faith. Let us not underestimate the Holy Spirit by thinking our children can get nothing

---

1. The Heidelberg Catechism says it like this: "Since, then, we are made partakers of Christ and all his benefits by faith only, whence comes this faith? The Holy Ghost works it in our heart by the preaching of the holy Gospel, and confirms it by the use of the holy Sacraments" (Q&A 65).

out of worship and preaching if it is not relevant and fun. The Holy Spirit is sovereign and irresistible, and cannot be frustrated by our limitations (John 3:1–8). And let us not underestimate our children, in whose minds and hearts the Holy Spirit is working.

Third, since worship is the most important thing we do in this life—our chief end being "to glorify God, and fully to enjoy him forever" (WLC, Q&A 1)—consider "the cumulative effect" of weekly worship services over the lifetime of your children. At the church I serve, the congregation gathers for worship in the morning and evening every Lord's Day.[2] Imagine the cumulative effect of this: two worship services every Lord's Day, for fifty-two weeks every year. That's 1,872 times your children will gather for worship from earliest infancy, through the formative years of childhood, and all the way through the teenage years before they go off to college at age eighteen.[3]

"But it is so hard to have my children in church with us." Yes it is, especially for those of us who did not grow up seeing this modeled for us. Think of it like this: is it easier to raise your children in church from infancy so that they are trained in it like everything else, or to put them in a separate class for several years, only to bring them into worship at a later time when they have never been in worship before? Experience shows that children who have been in some form of Sunday school or children's church, which for most churches means infancy through as late as twelve years of age, will be less prepared and trained to join in public worship than if they had spent those early and formative years next to their parents. Trying to get older children acclimated to something new that they have never done before is difficult. As one person said to me, a child is like clay, and the sooner you begin to mold it, the easier it is to shape; the longer you wait, the drier and harder it gets and vast potential of shaping it is lost. Our children's hearts and minds are like wet, malleable clay that we must begin to form as

2. On the evening service, see Clark, "Whatever Happened to the Second Service," 293–342; Sinnema, "Second Sunday Service."

3. For a great discussion of this cumulative effect, see *Family Worship Book*, 3–8.

soon as possible. As we read in the Scriptures, "Train up a child in the way he should go, and when he is old he will not depart from it" (Prov 22:6).

Fourth, including children in worship from an early age exposes them to the language of faith. Children are not only like wet clay, but also like dry sponges, able to absorb a tremendous amount. This is true even when our children say they are bored in worship. For many parents this is their greatest fear. Yet, when our children are in worship, the scriptural recitations, songs, creeds, and prayers become familiar. When they become familiar and memorable, our children are able to speak, sing, recite, and pray from the heart. The message of the songs we sing starts to sink in. The form of the service begins to feel natural. Even if most of the sermon goes over their heads when they are young, experience shows that children hear and remember remarkable things. The content of the prayers and songs and sermons gives parents unparalleled opportunities to teach their children the great truths of our faith.

We have a responsibility as parents to learn how to ask our children questions after the service and how to explain what was preached. In doing so, our children's capacity to participate in worship will soar. Not everything our children experience, then, has to be put "on their level." For example, in order to learn a new language, you can either go step by step from learning the alphabet to learning vocabulary to learning grammar to learning syntax; or, you can take a course that immerses you in a foreign world that is over your head. Yet contrary to what we would expect, learning by total immersion is by far the most effective method of learning a language.[4] By analogy, the same is true with teaching our children

4. For example, Colin Baker exposits more than one thousand studies on immersion programs and immersion language learners in Canada. These have resulted in a number of important points, which even apply to our topic: first, early immersion students (beginning at age five or six) lag behind their monolingual peers in literacy (reading, spelling, and punctuation) for the first few years only; second, early immersion students acquire native-like proficiency in passive skills (listening and reading) by the age of eleven. Baker, *Foundations of Bilingual Education.*

the language of the Christian faith through means of worship. Our children will grow to learn and love this new language as they join us in worship, and we as parents should be passionate for this.

The spiritual benefit the church of adults and children receives in worship can be described in these words: "Blessed is he who reads and those who hear the words of this prophecy, and keep those things which are written in it; for the time is near" (Rev 1:3). There is a blessing in the reading and hearing of the Word of God. Again, this would have occurred in the public service of the church in the first century. Christians did not have study Bibles as we do, but they would hear it read every Lord's Day. "The reading of the scriptures with godly fear . . . and conscionable hearing of the word, in obedience unto God, with understanding, faith, and reverence . . . are all parts of the ordinary religious worship of God" (WCF, 21.5).

I pray that as you reevaluate your understanding and position on this vital issue of our children in worship, not only will you come to include them, but also that your children will include theirs for generations to come. Together, may we experience the eternal benefits of the Son of God, which our heavenly Father offers us the nursery of the Holy Spirit.

Bibliography

Alexander, James W. *Thoughts on Family Worship*. Edited by Don Kistler. Morgan, PA: Soli Deo Gloria, 1998.

Anderson, J. R. *Learning and Memory: An Integrated Approach*. New York: Wiley, 1995.

Bacon, Richard. *Revealed to Babes: Children in the Worship of God*. Audubon, NJ: Old Paths, 1993.

Baker, Colin. *Foundations of Bilingual Education and Bilingualism*. 4th ed. Clevedon, England: Multilingual Matters, 2006.

Barna Research Group. "Teenagers Embrace Religion but Are Not Excited about Christianity." January 10, 2000. http://www.youth-ministry.info/articles.php5?type=2&cat=20&art_id=38.

Bastingius, Jeremias. *An Exposition or Commentarie Upon the Catechisme of Christian Religion Which Is Taught in the Schooles and Churches. . . .* John Legatt, 1589.

Beeke, Joel R. *Bringing the Gospel to Covenant Children in Dependency on the Spirit*. Grand Rapids: Reformation Heritage, 2001.

————. *The Family at Church: Listening to Sermons and Attending Prayer Meetings*. Grand Rapids: Reformation Heritage, 2008.

————. *Family Worship*. Grand Rapids: Reformation Heritage, 2005.

Best, Harold M. *Unceasing Worship: Biblical Perspectives on Worship and the Arts*. Downers Grove: InterVarsity, 2003.

Boling, Ruth. *Come Worship with Me: A Journey through the Church Year*. Louisville: Geneva Press, 2001.

Bosma, M. J. *Exposition of Reformed Doctrine*. 4th ed. Grand Rapids: Smitter, 1927.

Brown, Michael G. "A Cry for the Cry Room." *Christ United Reformed Church* blog, posted May 20, 2011. http://www.blog.christurc.org/2011/05/20/a-cry-for-the-cry-room.

Brueggemann, Walter. *The Creative Word: Canon as a Model for Biblical Education*. Minneapolis: Fortress, 1982.

Bibliography

Bullinger, Heinrich. *A Brief Exposition of the One and Eternal Testament or Covenant of Grace*. In *Fountainhead of Federalism: Heinrich Bullinger and the Covenantal Tradition*, translated by Charles S. McCoy and J. Wayne Baker. Louisville: Westminster John Knox, 1991.

Calvin, John. *Commentaries on the Book of Joshua*. Translated by Henry Beveridge. 22 vols. Grand Rapids: Baker, 1996.

———. *Commentaries on the Four Last Books of Moses: Arranged in the Form of a Harmony*. Vols. 1–2. Translated by Charles William Bingham. Grand Rapids: Baker, 1996.

———. *A Harmony of the Gospels, Matthew, Mark, and Luke*. Vol. 2. Translated by T. H. L. Parker. Edited by David W. Torrance and Thomas F. Torrance. Grand Rapids: Eerdmans, 1972.

———. *Institutes of the Christian Religion*. Edited by John T. McNeill. Translated by Ford Lewis Battles. 2 vols. Philadelphia: Westminster, 1960.

Campbell, Iain D. *On the First Day of the Week: God, the Christian, and the Sabbath*. Leominster, England: Day One, 2009.

Castleman, Robbie. *Parenting in the Pew*. Downers Grove: InterVarsity, 1993.

Christian Reformed Church. *Psalter Hymnal*. Grand Rapids: CRC Publications, 1976.

———. *Psalter Hymnal*. Grand Rapids: CRC Publications, 1988.

Clark, Neville. "Children and Worship." In *The New Westminster Dictionary of Liturgy and Worship*, edited by J. G. Davies, 161–63. Philadelphia: Westminster, 1986.

Clark, R. Scott. "Whatever Happened to the Second Service." In *Recovering the Reformed Confession*, 293–342. Phillipsburg, NJ: Presbyterian & Reformed, 2008.

———. "Why We Memorize the Catechism." *Presbyterian Banner*, August 2003.

"Constitutions of the Holy Apostles." In *Ante-Nicene Fathers*, vol. 7, edited by Alexander Roberts and James Donaldson, revised by A. Cleveland Coxe. 1886. Reprint, Peabody, MA: Hendrickson, 2004.

Cyprian. "The Unity of the Catholic Church." In *Early Latin Theology*, edited by S. L. Greenslade, 119–42. Louisville: Westminster, 1956.

De Boer, Erik A. "'O, Ye Women, Think of Thy Innocent Children, When They Die Young!' The Canons of Dordt (First Head, Article Seventeen) between Polemic and Pastoral Theology." In *Revisiting the Synod of Dordt (1618–1619)*, edited by Aza Goudriaan and Fred van Lieburg, 261–90. Leiden: Brill, 2011.

Dennison, James T., Jr. *The Market Day of the Soul: The Puritan Doctrine of the Sabbath in England 1532–1700*. 1983. Reprint, Grand Rapids: Reformation Heritage, 2008.

Geldenhuys, Norval. *The Gospel of Luke*. New International Commentary on the New Testament. Grand Rapids: Eerdmans, 1951.

Gispen, W. H. *Exodus*. Translated by Ed van der Maas. Student's Bible Commentary. Grand Rapids: Zondervan, 1982.

Hendriksen, William. *The Covenant of Grace*. Grand Rapids: Eerdmans, 1932.

Henry, Matthew. *Matthew Henry's Commentary on the Whole Bible.* Complete and unabridged in 1 vol. Peabody, MA: Hendrickson, 1991.

Hildersham, Arthur. *Dealing with Sin in Our Children.* Edited by Don Kistler. Lake Mary, FL: Soli Deo Gloria, 2004.

Horton, Michael. *God of Promise: Introducing Covenant Theology.* Grand Rapids: Baker, 2006.

House, Paul R. "Examining the Narrative of Old Testament Narrative: An Exploration in Biblical Theology." *Westminster Theological Journal* 67 (2005) 229–45.

Hyde, Daniel R. *Jesus Loves the Little Children: Why We Baptize Children.* Grandville, MI: Reformed Fellowship, 2012.

———. "The Little Parish." *Modern Reformation* 14 (2005) 20–24.

———. "A Primer on the Lord's Day." *Outlook* 59 (2009) 6–10.

———. *Welcome to a Reformed Church: A Guide for Pilgrims.* Orlando: Reformation Trust, 2010.

———. *What to Expect in Reformed Worship: A Visitor's Guide.* 2nd ed. Eugene, OR: Wipf & Stock, 2013.

Johnson, Terry L. *The Family Worship Book: A Resource Book for Family Devotions.* Ross-shire, UK: Christian Focus, 1998.

———, ed. *Leading in Worship.* Oak Ridge, TN: Covenant Foundation, 1996.

Kistler, Don, ed. *Sola Scriptura! The Protestant Position on the Bible.* Morgan, PA: Soli Deo Gloria, 1995.

Koelman, Jacobus. *The Duties of Parents.* Translated by John Vriend. Edited by M. Eugene Osterhaven. Grand Rapids: Baker Academic, 2003.

Lincoln, Andrew T. *Ephesians.* Word Biblical Commentary 42. Waco, TX: Word, 1990.

Lane, William L. *The Gospel of Mark.* New International Commentary on the New Testament. Grand Rapids: Eerdmans, 1974.

Marzano, Robert J., et al. *Classroom Instruction That Works: Research-Based Strategies for Increasing Student Achievement.* Alexandria, VA: Association for Supervision and Curriculum Development, 2001.

Muller, Richard A. *Dictionary of Latin and Greek Theological Terms: Drawn Principally from Protestant Scholastic Theology.* Grand Rapids: Baker, 1985.

Newell, A., and P. S. Rosenbloom. "Mechanisms of Skill Acquisition and the Law of Practice." In *Cognitive Skills and Their Acquisition*, edited by J. R. Anderson, 1–55. Hillsdale, NJ: Erlbaum, 1981.

Ng, David, and Virginia Thomas. *Children in the Worshipping Community.* Atlanta: John Knox, 1981.

Orthodox Presbyterian Church. *Trinity Hymnal.* Rev. ed. Norcross, GA: Great Commission, 1990.

Poole, Matthew. *A Commentary on the Whole Bible.* Vol. 1, *Genesis–Job.* Peabody, MA: Hendrickson, 2008.

Power, John Carroll. *The Rise and Progress of Sunday Schools: A Biography of Robert Raikes and William Fox.* New York: Sheldon, 1863.

Pronk, Cornelis. *Expository Sermons on the Canons of Dort.* St. Thomas, Ontario: Free Reformed, 1999.

Bibliography

Riddlebarger, Kim. "Squirming and Noisy Children of the Promise." Christ Covenant Church (Midland, MI) website. http://www.midlandpca.org/pdfs/squirming_children.pdf.

Ridgley, Thomas. *A Body Of Divinity: Wherein the Doctrines of the Christian Religion Are Explained and Defended* .... 4 vols. Philadelphia: Woodward, 1815.

Ryle, J. C. *Boys and Girls Playing (and Other Addresses to Children)*. Edited by Don Kistler. 1881. Reprint, Morgan, PA: Soli Deo Gloria, 1996.

Sandell, Elizabeth J. *Including Children in Worship: A Planning Guide for Congregations*. Minneapolis: Augsburg, 1991.

Sayers, Dorothy. "The Lost Tools of Learning." In *Recovering the Lost Tools of Learning: An Approach to Distinctively Christian Education*, edited by Douglas Wilson, 145–64. Wheaton, IL: Crossway, 1991.

Sinnema, Donald. "The Second Sunday Service in the Early Dutch Reformed Tradition." *Calvin Theological Journal* 32 (1997) 298–333.

Sproul, R. C. *The Consequences of Ideas: Understanding the Concepts That Shaped Our World*. Wheaton, IL: Crossway, 2000.

Ursinus, Zacharius. *The Commentary of Dr. Zacharius Ursinus on the Heidelberg Catechism*. Translated by G. W. Williard. 1852. Reprint, Phillipsburg, NJ: Presbyterian & Reformed, 1985.

Van Biema, David. "The New Calvinism." *Time*, March 12, 2009. http://content.time.com/time/specials/packages/article/0,28804,1884779_1884782_1884760,00.html.

Van Dyken, Donald. *Rediscovering Catechism: The Art of Equipping Covenant Children*. Phillipsburg, NJ: Presbyterian & Reformed, 2000.

Venema, Cornelis P. "The Election and Salvation of the Children of Believers Who Die in Infancy: A Study of Article I/17 of the Canons of Dort." *Mid-America Journal of Theology* 17 (2006) 57–100.

———. "The Lord's Supper and the 'Popish Mass': An Historical and Theological Analysis of Question and Answer 80 of the Heidelberg Catechism." *Mid-America Journal of Theology* 24 (2013) 31–72.

———. "The Lord's Supper and the 'Popish Mass': Does Q.&A. 80 of the Heidelberg Catechism Speak the Truth?" *Outlook* 55 (2005) 17–22.

Walker, Jeremy. "Attendance of Children in Public Worship." Banner of Truth website. July 11, 2002. http://banneroftruth.org/us/resources/articles/2002/attendance-of-children-in-public-worship.

Ward, Ruth McRoberts. *Worship Is for Kids, Too! The Why and How of Children's Worship*. Kalamazoo, MI: Masters, 1976.

Westerhoff, John, III. *Will Our Children Have Faith?* New York: Seabury, 1976.

Whitney, Donald S. *Family Worship: In the Bible, in History, and in Your Home*. Shepherdsville, KY: Center for Biblical Spirituality, 2005.

Worship & Rejoice. Hymnal. Carol Stream, IL: Hope, 2001.

Young, Edward J. *The Book of Isaiah*. Vol. 3, *Chapters 40–66*. 1972. Reprint, Grand Rapids: Eerdmans, 1996.

Scripture Index

GENESIS

3:1–7	7
3:8–9	8
3:14–19	8
3:15	8, 10
3:21	8
4:25	9
5:3	9
9:9	9, 10
9:9–17	8
11:10–26	9
11:27–12:1	9
13	9
15	8
15:4	8
17	8, 9
17:7	10
21:12	19
25:19–26:5	10
37:2	19
49:10	8

EXODUS

2:6	19
4:22–23	18
5:1	18
5:2	19
7:16	18
7–12	18
8:28	19
10:7–10	19
10:9	19
10:10	19
10:10–11	19
10:26	37
12–13	22
12:26–27	20
13:8, 14–15	21
13:14	21N9
19:1, 2	22
19:3	22
19:6	23
19:8	23
19:10–11	23
19–24	8
20:4	23
20:5–6	10, 23
20:8, 10	23
20:12	23
24	23

LEVITICUS

1–7	37

DEUTERONOMY

4	21n10
4:9–10	22n11
6:1–9	36
31:9–13	24
31:11	24
31:12	24
31:12–13	16

JOSHUA

8:30–35	23

1 SAMUEL

1:23, 25, 27	19

2 SAMUEL

7	8
7:13–14	8

2 CHRONICLES

20:3–5	25
20:13, 15	25

EZRA

9:2	33
10:1	16, 26

NEHEMIAH

8:1–3	16
8:2	26
12:27	27
12:43	27

PSALMS

2:11	40
8:2	xv, 39
51	53
78:1–8	39
95:2	44
100:1	xv
100:2	44
122:1	40
131	30

PROVERBS

22:6	59
31:28–29	xii

ISAIAH

6:13	33
7:14	8
53	8
54:13	17
60:1–4	17

JEREMIAH

31:31–34	8

DANIEL

9:24–27	8

MICAH

5:2	8

ZECHARIAH

8:5	18
8:23	40

MALACHI

3:1	8

MATTHEW

16	53
18–19	30
18:1	30
18:1–5	17
18:1–6	10
18:2–5	30
19.13–15	17, 28n20, 39
19:14	10
21:16	xv, xvn1

MARK

9:36–37	28
10	29, 30
10:1	27, 28
10:2–9	28
10:10–12	28
10:13	28
10:14–15	28
10:14–16	10, 39
10:16	29

LUKE

1:4	50n20
1:59, 2:17	28
2:46	20n7
3:22	8

7:32	28
18	30
18:15	29
18:15–17	10, 39
18:16–17	29

JOHN

3:1–8	58
12:31	8

ACTS

2:39	10, 56
2:42	41
18:25	50n20
21:21, 24	50n20

ROMANS

2:18	50n20
5:12–19	7
8:29	11
9:6	13
10:14–17	56
10:17	56
16:20	8

1 CORINTHIANS

7:14	10, 33

2 CORINTHIANS

12:9–10	33
14:19	50–51n20

GALATIANS

3:24	37
5:1	40
6:6	51n20

Scripture Index

EPHESIANS

1:1	31
1:3	31
1:4	31
1:6	32
1:7	31
1:9	31
1:10	31
1:11	31
1:12	31
1:13	31, 32
1:15	31
1:20	31
2:6	31
2:7	31
2:10	31
2:12	8
2:13	31
2:15	31
2:21	31, 32
2:22	32
3:6	31
3:11	31
3:12	32
3:13	32
4:17	31
4:20	31
4:32	31
5:8	31
6:1	31
6:1-4	16, 31
6:4	10, 36
6:10	31
6:21	31

COLOSSIANS

1:2	32
3:20	10, 16, 31, 32
4:16	32

HEBREWS

9:14-28	8
12:28-29	40
13:2	41
13:17	xvii

1 PETER

2:1-2	18
5:1-5	xvii

2 PETER

3:18	ix

3 JOHN

15	41

REVELATION

1:3	60
1:10	38
12	8
21:1-6	8
22:1-5	8

Confessions Index

BELGIC CONFESSION

Art. 29   xvii, 13
Art. 34   12

CANONS OF DORT

Head 1.17   9

HEIDELBERG
CATECHISM

Q&A 19   8
Q&A 65   57n1
Q&A 74   11
Q&A 80   5

WESTMINSTER
CONFESSION
OF FAITH

Ch. 7.5   8–9

Ch. 7.6   9
Ch. 21.5   60
Ch. 21.7   44
Ch. 25.2   11

WESTMINSTER
LARGER CATECHISM

Q&A 1   57
Q&A 31   9
Q&A 62   11
Q&A 116   44
Q&A 117   44
Q&A 154   56
Q&A 155   57
Q&A 166   11

WESTMINSTER
SHORTER CATECHISM

Q&A 59   44